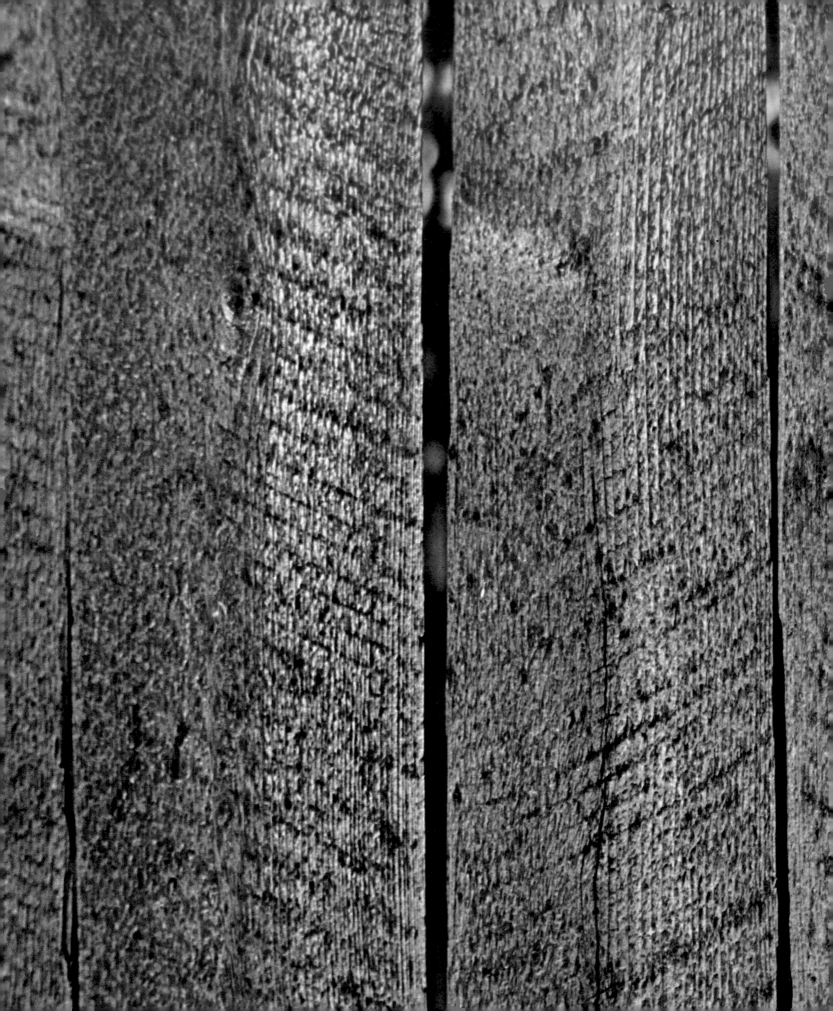

THE FAMILY CREATIVE WORKSHOP

14

Quilling, Quill Pens, Quilting
Raffia and Straw, Rag Dolls
Recycling Clothes
Repoussé and Chased Metal
Reverse Appliqué, Ribboncraft
Rockers and Cradles
Rope Knotting

Plenary Publications International, Inc.
New York and Amsterdam

Published by Plenary Publications International, Incorporated 300 East 40 Street, New York, N. Y. 10016, for the Blue Mountain Crafts Council.

Library of Congress Catalog Card Number: 73-89331. Complete set International Standard Book Number: 0-88459-021-6. Volume 14 International Standard Book Number: 0-88459-013-5.

Manufactured in the United States of America. Printed and bound by the W. A. Krueger Company, Brookfield, Wisconsin.

Printing preparation by Lanman Lithoplate Company.

Publishers:
Plenary Publications International, Incorporated
300 East 40 Street
New York, New York 10016

Steven Schepp
EDITOR-IN-CHIEF

Jerry Curcio
PRODUCTION MANAGER

Bonnie Schiffer
Peggy Streep
ADMINISTRATIVE ASSISTANTS

Editorial preparation:
Tree Communications, Inc.
250 Park Avenue South
New York, New York 10003

Rodney Friedman
EDITORIAL DIRECTOR

Ronald Gross
DESIGN DIRECTOR

Paul Levin
DIRECTOR OF PHOTOGRAPHY

Jill Munves
TEXT EDITOR

Sonja Douglas
ART DIRECTOR

Rochelle Lapidus
Marsha Gold
DESIGNERS

Lucille O'Brien
EDITORIAL PRODUCTION

Ruth Forst Michel
COPYREADER

Eva Gold
ADMINISTRATIVE MANAGER

Editors for this volume:
Andrea DiNoto
RAG DOLLS

Donal Dinwiddie
ROCKERS AND CRADLES

Michael Donner
ROPE KNOTTING

Linda Hetzer
RAFFIA AND STRAW
RECYCLING CLOTHES
RIBBONCRAFT

Nancy Bruning Levine
QUILTING
REVERSE APPLIQUÉ

Marilyn Nierenberg
REPOUSSÉ AND CHASED METAL

Mary Grace Skurka
QUILLING
QUILL PENS

Originating editor of the series:
Allen Davenport Bragdon

Contributing editors:
Lillian Gordon
Loretta Holz

Contributing photographer:
Stephen Mays

Contributing illustrators:
Marina Givotovsky
Lynn Matus
Sally Shimizu

Production:
Thom Augusta
Christopher Jones
Patricia Lee
Leslie Strong

Photo and illustration credits:
QUILLING : Photograph of antique quillwork sconce, page 1671, courtesy of the Metropolitan Museum of Art, New York, New York, gift of Mrs. Screven Lorillard, 1952; artificial Christmas tree, page 1675, courtesy of American Tree & Wreath, New York, New York. RAFFIA AND STRAW: Etchings, page 1711, courtesy of New York Public Library Picture Collection. REPOUSSÉ AND CHASED METAL: Sterling silver tray, courtesy of Gianmaria Buccellati, Inc., New York, New York; photograph of Coclé Indian plaque by Lisa Little, page 1745, courtesy of The Museum of Primitive Art, New York, New York. REVERSE APPLIQUÉ: *Molas,* pages 1755, 1757 and 1760, courtesy of Laurice Keyloun Boutique, White Plains, New York; contributing consultant: Pauline Antaki. RIBBONCRAFT: Etchings, page 1763, courtesy of New York Public Library Picture Collection. ROCKERS AND CRADLES: Painting, "The Hobby Horse," page 1775, courtesy of the National Gallery of Art, Washington, D.C.; photograph of King Charles I's rocking horse, page 1775, courtesy of Radio Times Hulton Picture Library, London, England.

The Project-Evaluation Symbols appearing in the title heading at the beginning of each project have these meanings:

Range of approximate cost:
¢ Low: under $5 or free and found natural materials

$ Medium: about $10

$$ High: above $15

Estimated time to completion for an unskilled adult:
⊠ Hours

🕐 Days

Weeks

Suggested level of experience:
Child alone

Supervised child or family project

Unskilled adult

Specialized prior training

Tools and equipment:
Small hand tools

Large hand and household tools

Specialized or powered equipment

On the cover:
Amber grain reflects the golden light of early morning. The head of wheat (center) is removed from the stalk (top), and the hollow straws that remain are flattened, braided, and coiled to make a straw hat (bottom). The braided hat was made by Ruth Straight Hibbs. See "Raffia and Straw" beginning on page 1710. Photograph by Paul Levin.

**Contents and
craftspeople for Volume 14:**

QUILLING
Paper Filigree

Quilling is the art of rolling, bending, and creasing narrow strips of paper into coils and scrolls, then assembling these shapes into two- and three-dimensional decorative designs. The shapes are usually set on edge so the inner curls show to best advantage. These delicate openwork designs resemble metal filigree or lace. The name, quilling, comes from the fact that the paper strips were at one time rolled on bird quills. Quilling dates back at least to the fifteenth century, when European nuns used narrow strips of paper cut from the edges of illuminated manuscripts to create delicate ornamentation for religious articles. The craft was brought to America by the women who settled in the colonies; they decorated such mundane household items as candle sconces and tea caddies with paper filigree. (The quilling that American Indians did was of another ilk; they decorated leather with porcupine and bird quills.)

Only a few examples of early quillwork survive today, such as the candle sconce shown at right. This scarcity is due in part to the fragile nature of the material, but quillwork probably was not handled carefully because it was not recognized for what it was; quilling done with gilt-edge paper resembled metal filigree, and cream-colored imitation parchment could have been mistaken for ivory or wood carvings.

The shapes used in quilling are quite stylized; yet the patterns they make range from simple, modern designs to ones that are very elaborate and intricate. The ultimate effect depends on the width, length, and thickness of the paper strips, the size and tightness of the shapes, and the colors and shadings of the papers. Quilling can be made into standing or hanging ornaments, or it can be attached to surfaces of blown-out eggs, boxes, picture frames, dollhouse furniture, and many other objects both decorative and useful.

Learning to roll the coils, the basic step in quilling, is quite simple if you have time, patience, and a liking for meticulous work done on a miniature scale. The rolling takes practice, and the trick is to keep the tension even. The creative part comes in choosing colors and shapes to arrange into flat, layered, and three-dimensional designs of infinite variety.

Materials and Tools

To do quillwork, you need narrow paper strips and a cardboard box in which to hang them in an orderly fashion (photograph 1, page 1672). You also need something to roll the strips on, such as a toothpick, and white liquid household glue (photograph 2, page 1672). Other helpful aids are: manicure scissors; tweezers for picking up small shapes; straight pins; a cup of water or a damp sponge for moistening strips and cleaning fingers; and an egg carton or muffin tin for sorting shapes. Your work surface should be a piece of beaver board or corrugated cardboard, about 9 by 18 inches, covered with a sheet of manila or other heavyweight paper with patterns drawn on it. Use waxed paper to cover the penciled patterns because neither paper lint nor glue sticks to its slick surface, but the patterns underneath it are clearly visible.

Precut quilling papers are offered in an assortment of colors at craft shops and in mail-order catalogs. Strips can be cut at home, but you need a good eye and a steady hand to cut them evenly. Quilling paper must be heavy enough to retain a shape, light enough to roll smoothly, resilient enough to spring open when uncoiled. You always cut the strips with the grain of the paper, so they can be rolled with the grain. To find the grain of a sheet of paper, roll it in both directions; it will roll more smoothly in one direction, which is with the grain.

The width of the paper strips is usually ⅛ inch, though it can be narrower, or it can be as wide as an inch for a loosely coiled shape. The bird of paradise on page 1682 is made entirely of 1/16-inch-wide strips. (To cut a ⅛-inch strip in half length-

Angela Lynch, wife of a Luverne, Minnesota farmer, has taught primary school and kindergarten for more than twenty years. Although she has long been interested in crafts, the quilling described here is a relatively recent preoccupation. Her work is sold in New York specialty shops and in several midwestern states.

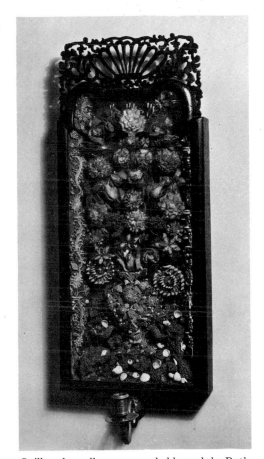

Quillwork candle sconce, probably made by Ruth Read of Redding, Connecticut around 1725, is one of a pair decorated with shells, wire filigree, and mica flowers in addition to the paper filigree. Each sconce measures 10⅞ by 28½ inches and holds a brass candle arm.

Quilled coils and scrolls, made of narrow strips of paper, are set on edge to give a delicate openwork effect often compared to lace or metal filigree. While the quilling shapes are standard, the finished designs vary greatly in the arrangement of these shapes and in the use of color.

By experimenting with the basic quilling shapes and various colors, you can learn to make recognizable flowers, birds, and butterflies, as well as abstract geometric designs.

1: Sort the narrow strips of quilling paper by color, and hang them over straight pins in a heavy cardboard box large enough to let them hang full length without bending. A box with a fold-in lid can be closed for storage.

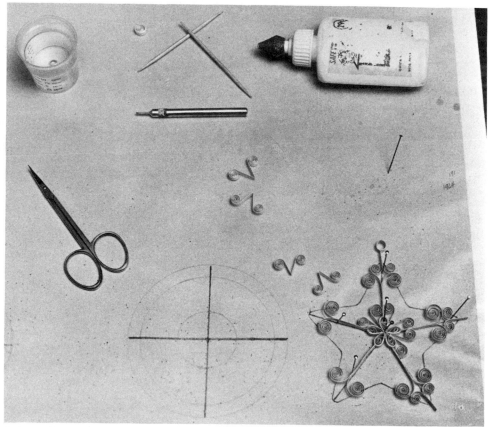

2: Assemble your quilling designs on beaver board or cardboard covered with waxed paper. Patterns slipped between will be clearly visible and will stay clean of paper lint and glue. Keep the following aids handy: manicure scissors; straight pins; a cup of water; white liquid glue with a toothpick applicator; and a rolling device—a metal quilling tool (shown) or a toothpick.

wise, use manicure scissors, and cut very slowly and carefully.) If you plan to frame quilled pieces, such as the butterflies on page 1678, or to make designs for greeting cards that you will mail, take the thickness of the coils into consideration so they won't be crushed. Occasionally commercially cut papers will vary slightly in width, and papers of various colors will vary in weight. These differences do not matter in most projects, but you should be aware of the possibilities.

Most quilling shapes are made with strips 2 to 8 inches long. Practice making different shapes to see how much paper each takes. Keep a record of the lengths used for each size, and when you make a design requiring two or more identical shapes, cut the strips equal length. (Draw lines, equaling the most used lengths, on your work surface; such a guide is quicker to use than a ruler.)

As the basic quilling tool, you can use anything from a round pencil or knitting needle to a feather quill or No. 3 insect pin, depending on the design you want. The thinner the quilling tool, the smaller the hole in the center of the coil will be. This smaller hole assures a more delicate look, while a larger hole is appropriate for a loose, open design. The most common quilling tools are a round wooden toothpick tapered at the ends, a corsage pin with a large bead head, or a special quilling tool made of metal.

The toothpick works fine for beginners; in fact, the texture of the wood helps hold the paper strip. With a toothpick, you make the coil by turning the toothpick, not the paper. Squeeze the end tightly around the toothpick, and roll the first few turns slowly. Roll the toothpick toward you with your right hand while you hold the paper lightly with your left hand to keep the coil from slipping (photograph 3). (If you are left-handed, roll with your left and hold with your right hand.) The tapered shape of the toothpick permits variations in the tightness of the center coil, depending upon where on the toothpick you roll the strip. If you use a corsage pin or other metal pin or needle, the tool acts only as an axis around which the strip is wound; the paper itself is turned while the pin remains stationary. A tool designed for quilling makes rolling easier by holding the beginning of the paper strip, but the crimp it puts in the paper may be undesirable in your design.

You can also roll coils without a tool, using only your fingers. This is the best way to achieve a very tight center, but it is somewhat difficult to avoid squeezing the coils out of shape.

If you have difficulty starting a coil, dampen the end of the paper strip, and moisten your fingertips slightly. (If your fingers are too wet or are sticky with glue, the paper will lose the crispness that is part of the beauty of quillwork.) For best results, maintain an even tension on the paper. Too little tension will let the center start unwinding before the coil is finished; too much tension will result in a coil that will not open evenly or as wide as you might like. The end that will be on the outside may be torn to make that edge less visible. The outer end can also be cut if it will be hidden by another shape.

Only a tiny drop of clear-drying white glue is needed to secure a shape when it has reached the size desired and to join the shapes wherever they touch. Always glue closed coils to size before pinching them into other shapes. Scrolls are generally not glued until they are put into a design. Lay the glue bottle on its side to keep the glue flowing smoothly, and squeeze a drop onto a toothpick applicator as you need it. Put another toothpick on the work surface to act as a rest for the glue applicator when it is not in use (photograph 2).

Assembling the Design

Patterns for the flat designs in the following projects are given full size; trace them onto heavy paper to slip under the waxed paper of your work surface. Roll the coils and scrolls the pattern calls for, pinning them in place over the pattern with straight pins, and glue them together wherever they touch. When a design is to have a background, you can work directly on that surface, gluing each shape in place as it is made. Or you can construct the entire unit first; then glue it to the background. When you work with a curved surface such as that of an egg, it is best to work directly on the egg. You can arrange shapes on your work surface without gluing them together until you find a pleasing arrangement; then transfer them one by one to the egg. When you are creating your own designs, it helps to make patterns of concentric circles of various diameters and intersecting lines to serve as guides (photograph 2).

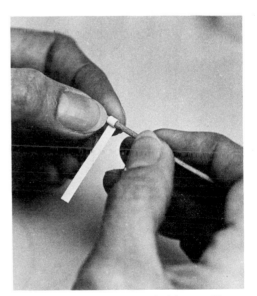

3: When you use a wooden toothpick as a rolling tool, roll the toothpick toward you with your right hand, and gently hold the paper with your left. The texture of the toothpick helps hold the inside end of the paper strip. When you use a metal corsage pin as a tool, roll the paper itself around the stationary tool, which acts as an axis.

CRAFTNOTES: BASIC QUILLING

There are two basic shapes you can make with quilling—coils and scrolls. These can be loose or tight, and pinched, bent, or creased into various shapes. Tight shapes are glued without being allowed to unwind. Loose shapes are allowed to unwind to the size desired before glue is applied.

Coils

Tight coil:
Roll a coil from one end of the paper strip and glue the outside end without letting it unwind. It will stay better if you hold it closed for a few seconds after it has been rolled; then glue it.

Loose coil:
Roll a coil from one end of the paper strip; then let it unwind to the size you want before you glue the outside end.

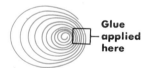

Glue applied here

Off-center coil:
Roll a loose coil and pull the center to one side with a straight pin. Add a drop of glue to the edges between the center and the outermost edge.

Teardrop:
Roll a loose coil, glue the outer end, then pinch one side of the coil and leave the other side rounded.

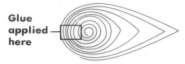

Glue applied here

Off-center teardrop:
Make a teardrop and pull the center toward the rounded end with a straight pin; then add a drop of glue to the edges between the center and the rounded edge.

Petal:
Make a teardrop and bend the pointed end slightly to one side.

Pressed heart:
Roll a loose coil, then pinch one end and indent the round end with your fingernail to get a heart shape.

Marquise or diamond:
Roll a loose coil and pinch both ends between thumb and forefinger. (Make a leaf shape by bending both pinched ends of a marquise in opposite directions.)

Holly leaf:
Make a marquise shape with two end points; then push these points to the center, creating points on the sides. This shape is best when it is uneven.

Half moon:
Roll a loose coil and pinch it so it has two end points and an indentation on one side.

Scrolls

Double scroll:
Roll both ends loosely toward the center on the same side of the paper strip. The coils meet in the center of the scroll.

S-shaped scroll:
Roll both ends to the center on opposite sides of the strip, leaving a short connecting strip between the two coils. Curl into an S shape.

V-shaped scroll:
Fold the strip in half and roll both ends to the outside.

One-sided V scroll:
Fold the strip so you have two uneven ends; then roll both ends loosely in the same direction.

Inward scroll or heart:
Fold the strip in half and roll both ends to the inside until they meet.

Relaxed or open scroll:
Roll a loose coil and stretch the outside end to the desired length.

Christmas tree ornaments destined to become family treasures are quilled in traditional colors. Pat terns for ornaments shown above and on page 1670 are given in Figure A, pages 1676 and 1677.

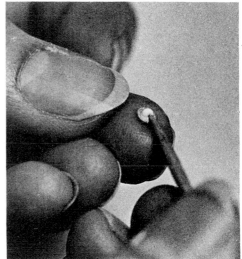

4: To apply a rhinestone to any design, put a tiny drop of glue on the flat back of the stone.

5: Use the toothpick to flip the stone over, and slide it into position on the quilled shape.

Paper Folding and Cutting
Holiday ornaments ¢ ▨ 🏃 🎁

Next holiday season, deck your tree with a tiny wreath, many different snowflakes guaranteed not to melt, a shy angel, and a miniature Christmas tree, all made of paper strips quilled to intricate laciness. Full-sized patterns for the ornaments pictured above and on page 1670 are given in Figure A on pages 1676 and 1677; follow both the patterns and the photographs if you want to duplicate the quilling shapes and the color combinations.

The angel is about 4 by 5 inches, the tree is 4 by 4½ inches, the wreath (page 1670) is 2½ inches in diameter, and the snowflakes range from 2 to 3½ inches across.

The angel and the Christmas tree are decorated with shiny rhinestones to reflect light. To attach a rhinestone, use a toothpick to put a drop of glue onto the back (photograph 4). Then use the toothpick to flip the rhinestone over and slide it to the position indicated on the pattern (photograph 5). The tree has rhinestones on both sides. Decorate one side; then turn the piece over and decorate the other side. The other ornaments may be similarly decorated if you like.

The angel's halo is a single circle of paper slipped over the head and glued in place. Wings are simple loops made by gluing the ends of strips together and joining them to the body.

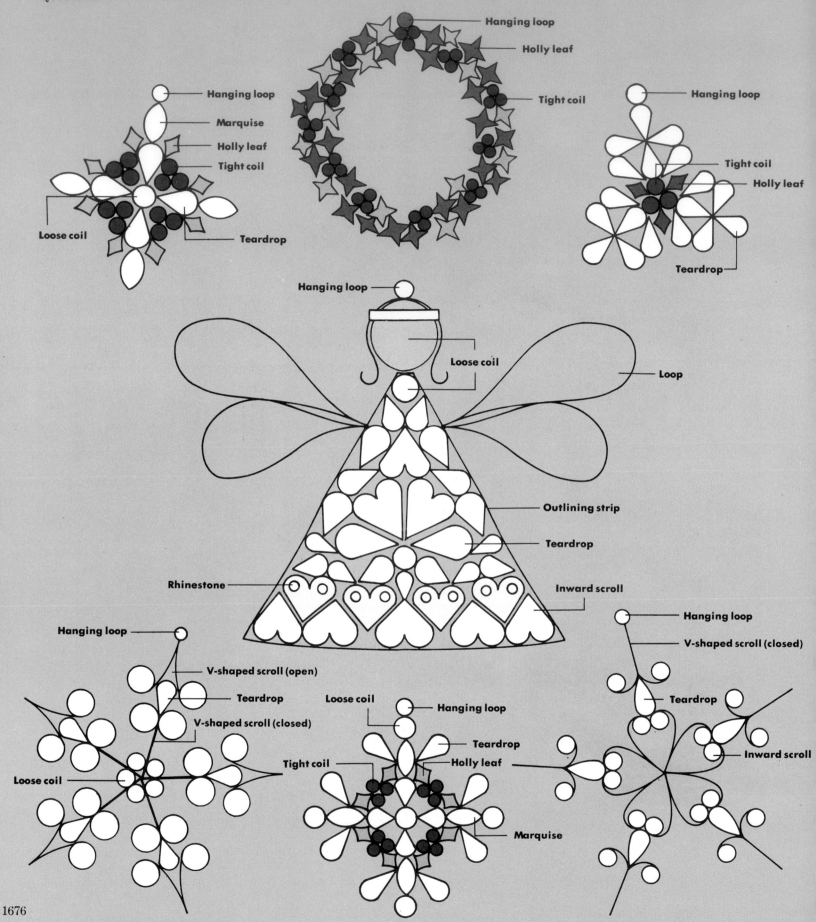

Hanging loop

Holly leaf

Tight coil

Hanging loop

Marquise

Holly leaf

Tight coil

Loose coil

Teardrop

Hanging loop

Tight coil

Holly leaf

Teardrop

Hanging loop

Loose coil

Loop

Outlining strip

Teardrop

Rhinestone

Inward scroll

Hanging loop

V-shaped scroll (open)

Teardrop

V-shaped scroll (closed)

Loose coil

Loose coil

Hanging loop

Tight coil

Teardrop

Holly leaf

Marquise

Hanging loop

V-shaped scroll (closed)

Teardrop

Inward scroll

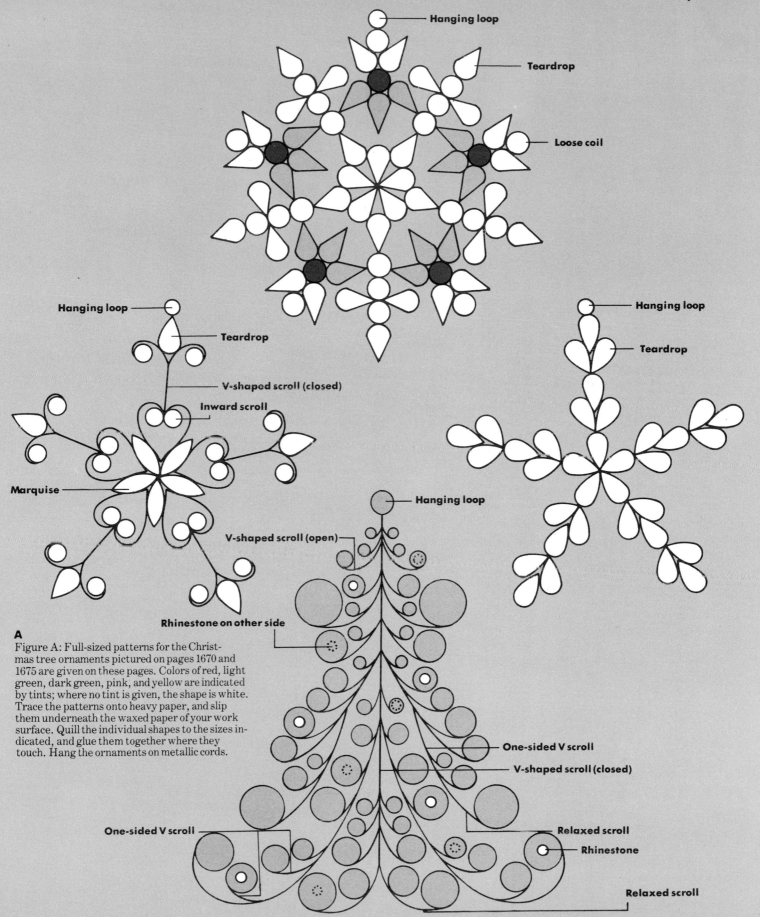

Hanging loop

Teardrop

Loose coil

Hanging loop

Teardrop

Hanging loop

Teardrop

V-shaped scroll (closed)

Inward scroll

Marquise

Hanging loop

V-shaped scroll (open)

Rhinestone on other side

A

Figure A: Full-sized patterns for the Christmas tree ornaments pictured on pages 1670 and 1675 are given on these pages. Colors of red, light green, dark green, pink, and yellow are indicated by tints; where no tint is given, the shape is white. Trace the patterns onto heavy paper, and slip them underneath the waxed paper of your work surface. Quill the individual shapes to the sizes indicated, and glue them together where they touch. Hang the ornaments on metallic cords.

One-sided V scroll

V-shaped scroll (closed)

One-sided V scroll

Relaxed scroll

Rhinestone

Relaxed scroll

Six charming butterflies are fine examples of how color can be used to give dimension and shading to flat quillwork. The grouping can be framed in a plastic box frame, as pictured, or mounted under glass (with clearance) for a coffee-table top. Individual butterflies could also be embedded in clear acrylic plastic for coasters or paperweights. Full-sized patterns for wings and bodies are given in Figures B and C, below and opposite.

Paper Folding and Cutting
Butterfly collection

The six quillwork butterflies pictured above are as pretty as real ones but much easier to collect. They are similar to the holiday ornaments in the preceding project in that they are flat shapes only ⅛ inch thick. But the butterflies are much more varied and subtle in color, with as many as six different shades in one wing. If you like, try your own combinations of colors, following photographs of real butterflies or letting your imagination take flight. Patterns for large and small butterfly bodies are given below (Figure B). Each full-sized pattern in Figure C, opposite, is for one wing; turn the pattern over when you make the matching wing. The largest yellow butterfly is about 5 by 6 inches; the two smaller yellow butterflies are 3½ by 4½ inches and 4½ by 3¼ inches. The blue butterfly is 2½ by 4¼ inches; the pink one is 2¾ by 4¼ inches; the purple butterfly is 4½ by 3¼ inches.

Whether you make just a couple of butterflies or a whole collection, mount them on background paper or fabric with a drop or two of glue before you frame them in either a plastic box frame (the one above is 11½ by 14 inches) or in a conventional glass-front picture frame. Be sure to allow ⅛-inch clearance to avoid crushing the quilling.

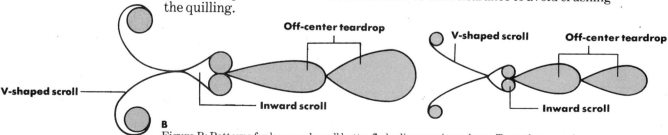

Figure B: Patterns for large and small butterfly bodies are given above. Trace them onto heavy paper, and use as guides when you quill the shapes needed. The larger body is for the large yellow butterfly; the smaller body is for the other five butterflies. Both bodies are black.

Loose coil

Purple butterfly

Off-center teardrop

Off-center petal

Petal

Loose coil

Small yellow butterfly

Off-center teardrop

Petal

Off-center teardrop

Large yellow butterfly

Off-center teardrop

Off-center teardrop

Half moon

Loose coil

Petal

Off-center petal

Half moon

Off-center teardrop

Half moon

Off-center teardrop

Off-center teardrop

Loose coil

Medium yellow butterfly

Off-center teardrop

Pink butterfly

Off-center coil

Loose coil

Off-center petal

Half moon

Blue butterfly

C

Figure C: Full-sized patterns for the wings of the six butterflies pictured opposite have color values as well as shapes indicated. The colors are graduated from palest blue (corresponding to the lightest value of the color range you select) to dark purple (the deepest value). Trace each pattern onto heavy paper, and quill the shapes to fit. Turn each pattern over when you make the matching wing. When both wings and the body are completed, glue them together.

Eggs decorated with delicate quilling brighten the Easter breakfast table. Clusters of pastel flowers cover almost every inch of the blown-out eggshells; a few scrolls crown the tops.

Eggs are ornamental for Christmas, too, when they are decorated with traditional motifs. Only a few basic quilling shapes are needed to make the wreath, tree, and holly designs.

Paper Folding and Cutting
Eggs for Easter and Christmas ¢ ▨ 👫 🦐

Blown-out eggs covered with quillwork offer a three-dimensional way to display your quilling talents. Decorate eggs for Easter with clusters of pastel floral shapes, and set them on small metal egg stands or other decorative holders from a craft shop. Red and green designs incorporating holly leaf, wreath, and tree shapes make the eggs suitable to hang on thin metallic cords as Christmas ornaments.

To blow out an eggshell, first puncture both ends with the tip of one blade of manicure scissors (the holes will be hidden by quilling or the stands). Insert a needle through one hole to break the yoke. Hold the egg over a bowl and blow out the contents. Rinse the inside of the egg, and let it dry. Paint the outside of the eggshell with several coats of clear nail polish to give it a shine and to keep it from cracking.

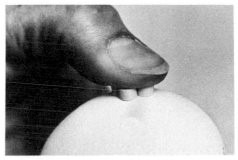

6: When you apply quilled shapes to an eggshell, transfer them onto the egg one at a time, without first gluing them together. Plan your design right on the egg or follow a pattern.

7: After several shapes have been glued to the egg, hold them firmly under your thumb for a few seconds to be sure they are securely attached. Be careful--the egg is fragile.

Quill the decorative shapes, and glue them in place with clear-drying white glue. Either work directly on the surface of the egg or plan the design on a pattern grid; then transfer the individual pieces to the egg (photograph 6). Do not attempt to assemble a complete glued unit that you will then transfer to the egg; the flat pieces will not conform to the curved surface. When you have glued several shapes to an egg, press them down with your thumb for a few seconds to make sure they are secure (photograph 7).

A decorative design that helps you space the motifs evenly is made with paper strips that divide the egg into lengthwise segments. This was done on the lavender Easter egg and all three Christmas eggs pictured. Glue these strips in place before attaching the quilled shapes.

Paper Folding and Cutting
Bird of paradise ¢ 🕐 👤 🦐

The fantasy bird pictured on page 1682, an example of free-standing, three-dimensional quillwork, could be used as a table centerpiece or be displayed on a bookshelf. The bird is 6 inches tall and about 6 inches long from bill to tail. It is perched on an oval wooden base decorated with exotic-looking flowers and vines. The bird is made of six shades of blue quilling paper, with all strips cut to a 1/16-inch width. Eyes are off-white teardrops, centered with gold-colored rhinestones. The bill is a pale yellow petal shape.

Assemble the body, about 2¾ inches long, on a poly-resin dome (the kind used for découpage and dome art) from a craft shop to give it a slight curve (photograph 8, page 1683). Draw the outline of the overall shape you want, basically an oval, and fill it in with quilled teardrop shapes. Make one side of the body first; then reverse the design for the opposite side. When both sides are complete, join them with additional quilling shapes on the top of the bird's back for more width there. Join the bottom (the bird's breast) without added quilling shapes except where they are needed to fill gaps.

This exotic bird of paradise, poised for flight on a flower-covered base, has a hollow body and head and stands on paper-wrapped wire legs. A pattern for the layered wing is given in Figure D.

A front view of the bird shows the curvature of the body and head and the placement of the eyes and bill.

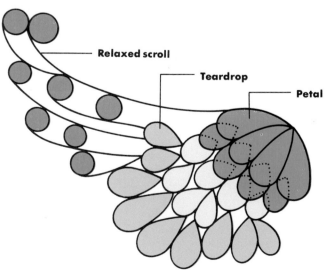

D

Figure D: A full-sized pattern for the bird's wing is given above, with color values and quilling shapes keyed. The dotted lines indicate the overlapping of teardrop shapes that gives dimension. Turn the pattern over when you make the other wing.

1682

Quill the head, also made of teardrop shapes, around a seed pod, marble, or other globular object to give it roundness; remove the pod before the underside is glued together. Make the neck of three loose coils stacked and glued together; then cover it completely with uneven double scrolls in several shades of blue. These scrolls give the bird its feathered look.

A full-sized pattern for one wing is given in Figure D; turn the pattern over for the second wing. Assemble the wings on a flat surface (photograph 9), but layer them at the rounded ends to give them depth; then attach them to the body at an angle so the relaxed scrolls at the end rise above the body. Make the tail of relaxed scrolls as well.

Make the long legs and feet of covered craft wire. The legs are two strands of wire twisted together and around the feet; the feet are two single wires twisted together (Figure E). With brown quilling paper, wrap both the legs and feet in a spiral (photograph 10). Slip the legs through openings in the underside of the body, and secure them with several small strips of paper glued to both body and legs. Cover these joinings with double scrolls for a feathered effect similar to that of the neck. Glue the bird to the base and surround his feet with flowers and vines.

For related crafts and entries, see "Lace," "Origami," and "Quill Pens."

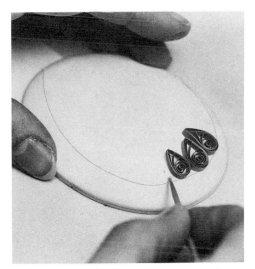

8: The body of the bird is made in two parts that are joined with additional quilling shapes. Draw the basic oval shape on a poly-resin dome, available at craft shops, and fill in the outline with teardrops of several sizes and shades of blue.

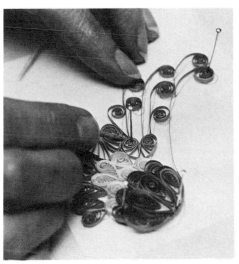

9: The bird's wing is made up of teardrops, petals, and relaxed scrolls in several shades of blue. Following the pattern opposite, assemble the wing on a flat surface, but layer the first three rows at the rounded end to give added dimension.

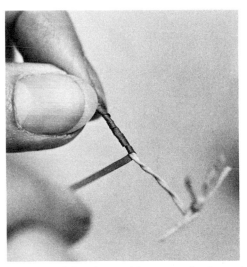

10: The bird's long legs and feet are made of coated craft wires twisted together (Figure E, below) and covered with spirals of brown quilling paper. The legs are inserted into the hollow body, and the joinings are covered with scrolls.

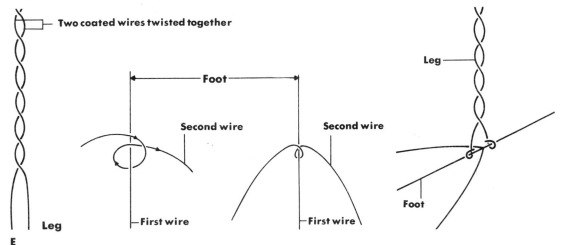

Two coated wires twisted together

Foot

Second wire   **Second wire**

Leg

Leg   **First wire**   **First wire**   **Foot**

E

Figure E: Each of the bird's legs (left) is made of two long lengths of wire twisted together. Each foot (center left and center right) has two short wires twisted together. Join a leg to a foot (right), and wrap the assembly with brown quilling paper (photograph 10).

QUILL PENS
Mightier than the Sword

Did you know that the single-bladed pocketknife, still called a penknife occasionally, was designed as a tool for cutting and mending quill pens? Or that stationery stores got their name from the men who stationed themselves on street corners to repoint and sharpen quill pens and sell related supplies? Quill pens were the main writing instruments from some time prior to the seventh century, when they were mentioned in the writings of Saint Isidore of Seville, until the middle of the nineteenth century, when they were replaced by more durable steel pen points in wooden holders. This modernization was not entirely an improvement, though. From the standpoint of everyday calligraphy, it is hard to imagine any penmanship that can compare with the beautiful flowing script created by a writer with a quill pen.

Selecting the Quill

The quills used for pens are usually the hollow shafts of large wing feathers from birds such as geese and turkeys, although quills of other large and medium-sized birds, including crows, swans, sea gulls, and even the tail feathers of male pheasants, can be used (photograph 1). The two-toned feather that looks as though it came from an eagle (photograph 2) is a white goose feather partially colored with

John Harnish, Jr. has a marketing and communications consulting firm in Lancaster, Pennsylvania. A native of that area, he is active in community affairs, especially the Chamber of Commerce and the Jaycees. From his childhood he can remember watching his grandfather, a printer, cut quill pens.

The men who signed the Declaration of Independence did so with a flourish of quill pens, lending visual distinction to a documentation of ideas that have shaped the world.

1: A wing feather from a goose (top) or a turkey (center) is most often used for making a quill pen, but the long tail feather of a male pheasant (bottom) can be used to make an unusual pen.

2: This two-toned feather that looks as though it might have come from an eagle is really a white goose feather dipped for about three-quarters of its length into brown liquid fabric dye.

3: Feathers can be classified in two groups, those with wide, open tips on the shaft (left) and those with tapered, almost closed tips (right). The latter are preferred for pen making.

brown liquid fabric dye. (The black feather in photograph 4, page 1686, is a dyed feather from a white goose.)

The choice feathers for pen making are the first four at the outside edge of the wing. Of these, the first is the finest. Feathers with narrow, almost closed tips are preferable for pen making to those with open tips (photograph 3). Feathers can also be categorized on the basis of whether they came from a right or left wing (photograph 4, page 1686). If you are right-handed and will hold the pen with the front

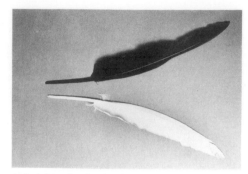

4: A right-wing feather (top) is better suited for a left-handed person and a left-wing feather (bottom) is better for a right-handed person.

5: The outer cuticle of a feather shaft, below the barbs, is hard, shiny, and smooth. Where the barbs start is a small tuft of down.

(smooth) side on top, as is traditional, a feather from a left wing will nestle nicely into the curve of your hand; if you are left-handed, choose a feather from a right wing. Of course, you can hold the feather with the back (dented) side upward if that is more comfortable. In that case, select a feather from the right wing if you are right-handed and from the left wing if you are left-handed.

If you don't know a poultry breeder who will give you moulted feathers, ask your county extension service for the names of some in your area. Other sources include poultry markets, zoo aviaries, and feather suppliers. Three such suppliers of cleaned white goose feathers are: Jacob Baum, P. O. Box 54, Strasburg, Pennsylvania 17579; Creatus, P. O. Box 6124, Lancaster, Pennsylvania 17603; and Ellen Schultz Associates, 7 Cricket Lane, Westport, Connecticut 06880. Do not attempt to pluck the feathers from live birds.

Tools, Old and New

All you need to shape a quill pen is a penknife or a sharp craft knife with a short angled blade. When pen making was a common pursuit, there were more elaborate tools, including clippers, cutters, slitters, and combinations of these in pocket-sized cases. You may chance upon such tools, as well as inkwells, in antique shops.

Environmental Projects
A feather in the hand

The first step in making a quill pen is cleaning the feather. If the feathers you use are fresh, scald the tips in boiling water for a few minutes to remove any oily or fatty materials that would interfere with the flow of ink. Then let the feathers dry thoroughly—at least overnight—before cutting. Another method of cleaning, used by the Dutch centuries ago and still effective, is that of inserting the feather tips into hot sand (140 degrees Fahrenheit) for several minutes. This technique cleans and whitens the tips of the shafts.

The transparent cuticle at the large end of the feather shaft is hard, smooth, and shiny (photograph 5), but it can be easily peeled away with your thumbnail (photograph 6). On the back of the shaft, there is a lengthwise dent filled with pith

A quill pen can be used to make delicate drawings as well as for writing powerful words. The classic quill, pictured, comes from a white goose. Search antique shops and flea markets for a pretty inkwell, such as the one above, to complement it.

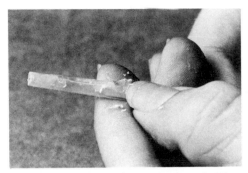

6: The transparent cuticle must be cleaned off before the pen can be cut. You can easily peel it away with your thumbnail.

7: The lengthwise dent on the back side of the shaft must be scraped clean of pith with your thumbnail or a dull blade.

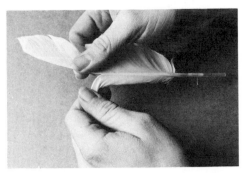

8: The feather barbs on either side of the shaft can be removed simply by pulling downward from the point, if you prefer that look.

9: If the feather you use is a fresh one, you must clean it, then cut off the tapered tip before you make any of the shaping cuts.

10: Once the tip is cut off, you can clean out the pith inside the hollow shaft with the point of your knife blade.

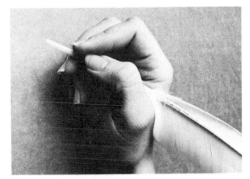

11: Before making any shaping cuts, hold the feather in your hand to find the most comfortable position for writing or drawing.

(photograph 7); clean this out with your nail or a dull blade. After the initial cuts are made, you will also clean out the pith inside the barrel of the feather.

You may find that you prefer quill pens stripped clean of feather barbs on one lengthwise side. You can easily pull these barbs, collectively called a blade, away from the shaft of the feather in one continuous piece if you start at the outside tip of the feather (photograph 8). Feathers with blades of unequal width are called pointers; those with equal blades are called broad or round feathers.

Hold the quill firmly on a hard, smooth surface, and cut off the shaped end tip of the shaft (photograph 9). Clean out the pith inside (photograph 10).

Before you make any shaping cuts, hold the feather in your hand as you will hold the finished pen (photograph 11). Since you will be custom-cutting the pen, you might as well make it as comfortable as you can. Do not worry about crushing the feathers in the cutting process—they are very resilient. When you find a comfortable position for the pen to rest in your hand, rotate the feather so that the underside will be on top in preparation for cutting.

Make the first cut a vertical one, halfway through the shaft, about ½ inch from the tip (photograph 12, page 1688). Next, make a horizontal cut from the end of the shaft to meet the vertical cut, creating a scooped out section (photograph 13, page 1688). At this point you can also remove any additional pith that might be inside the shaft. Next, make a straight, even slit through the center of the nib as a reservoir to hold a supply of ink. To make a smooth slit, cut slowly and carefully for the entire length of the nib (photograph 14, page 1688).

Secondary cuts, called sloping the shoulders, taper the sides of the nib to meet at the slit in the center (photograph 15, page 1688). It is better to make the slit before you taper the sides to give yourself a center point to aim at. Do not worry about making the nib pretty—it need only be pointed and able to hold ink.

At this stage the quill already looks like a steel penpoint. By tapering the sides, you also shorten the length of the nib. If the nib is too long, the pen tip will be too soft, and you will need to shorten the slit by cutting away more of the sides. If the slit is too short, the point will usually be too hard to write well; then you will need to

An advertisement for a Philadelphia quill pen merchant offered swan and crow quills, as well as ink powder and sealing wax in many colors.

12: The first shaping cut is a vertical one on the underside of the shaft. It should be made halfway through, about ½ inch from the tip.

13: The next cut is made horizontally from the tip to the vertical cut. This creates a scooped-out section on the underside of the shaft.

14: Without turning the feather over, make a full-length slit in the center of the nib section. Keep it as straight and even as possible.

15: Gradually taper both sides of the nib, a bit at a time, to meet at the center slit. This procedure is called sloping the shoulders.

16: With several short, slight cuts, further refine the shape of the nib and the scoop to suit your writing or drawing needs.

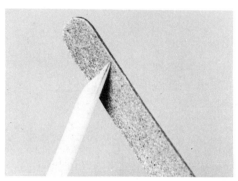

17: Finally, with the finishing side of an emery board or very fine sandpaper, smooth any rough spots from the cut edges of the pen.

lengthen the slit and perhaps recut the scooped-out section. If you make a mistake, simply cut off the shaped part of the tip and start again—most quills are long enough to permit two complete cuttings.

Finally, refine the nib to suit your writing or drawing purpose (photograph 16 and Figures A, B, and C). Cut away the corners of the scoop in small, short cuts—do not attempt to cut them perfectly with a single stroke. Then hold the blade perpendicular to the quill, and cut off the very tip of the nib if that is desirable. This operation is called cross nibbing. If you prefer a more flexible point, shave a slight bit off the top side of the nib.

With frequent use, the nib of a quill pen will wear down in three or four months. To recut it, slope the shoulders and renib the point, just as you did originally. The slit will not need to be lengthened each time a new point is cut, but when that does become necessary, lengthen it the same way you cut the original slit.

You may wish to smooth all the cut edges of the quill pen with a fine emery board (photograph 17). If any of the feathers are crushed from handling, steam them over boiling water to restore their fullness.

Before each use, put your quill pen in water for 15 minutes to eliminate brittleness, making the nib more flexible. Then dip the pen into an ink bottle or inkwell. Do not scrape it against the side to remove excess ink—that would damage the point. Let the ink drain back until the point does not drip. A dark ink is a traditional choice, but any free-flowing colored ink or thinned water-color paint will work.

To get the feel of the pen in your hand, try some practice strokes before writing a letter or starting a drawing. Writing with a quill pen is different from writing with any other kind of pen. You will be more conscious of your handwriting and will probably be more careful as you form the letters. Try to maintain a featherlight touch; this will give better results than heavy pressure. Downstrokes are usually easier and smoother than upstrokes; the latter can cause a drag on the point. Quill pens need frequent refilling with ink to maintain an even flow.

For related crafts, see "Calligraphy," "Folk Art," "Papermaking," and "Quilling."

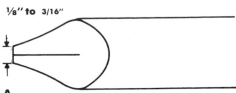

A

Figure A and photograph, left: To cut a pen suitable for bold, broad strokes of calligraphy, shape the nib so that it is short and stubby. As shown, the nib is cut straight across; other effects can be achieved with angled cuts.

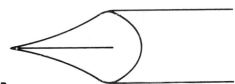

B

Figure B and photograph, left: To make a pen with a fine point suitable for line drawings and illustrations, taper the nib to a long, slender point and do not cut off the point. Use very light pressure to avoid bending the nib.

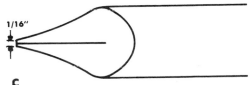

C

Figure C and photograph, left: To cut a pen with a medium point that is useful for general writing and the thinner accent lines of calligraphy, taper the nib to a slender point; then cross nib the point to a width of about 1/16 inch.

QUILTING
From Rags to Riches

Potholders and sleeping bags may seem an unlikely pair, but they are related—and the word quilted tells you how.

Quilting is the process used to hold together layers of fabric by sewing a series of small stitches through the layers. Usually there are three such layers: a top, a bottom (the backing), and a filling. Today, the middle layer usually is a soft, fluffy, thick substance called batting that provides efficient insulation from heat (as in potholders) and cold (as in sleeping bags). It is also useful where extra thickness, body, and padding are needed; long ago quilted garments were worn under, and sometimes substituted for, military armor.

Quilting has long been popular in China, India, Iran, Egypt, and some areas of Africa. The Crusaders took quilting to Europe when they returned from Asia wearing quilted undergarments. Quilting (particularly of bedcovers, which have come to be called quilts because of a long association with this technique) reached the status of a minor art in Europe in the fourteenth century, which had the coldest winters in the modern history of that continent. Portions of one of the oldest surviving quilts, made in Sicily around 1400, are preserved in the Victoria and Albert Museum, London, and in the Bargello in Florence. By the seventeenth century, quilted bedcovers and clothing reached a high level of popularity that lasted for two centuries. Many fine examples date from this period.

From Europe, quilting and quilt designs traveled to North America. The first American quilts were patchwork—patches of fabric sewn together to form one large piece. Many of these quilts were crazy quilts, patchwork with no particular pattern or design, made with fabric scraps of random size, shape, and color. Eventually, individualistic pioneers added design characteristics that reflected their own tastes, needs, and materials. Although patchwork and appliqué (stitching small fabric pieces to a larger piece of background fabric) probably did not originate in America, most of the designs embellishing today's handmade quilts stem from the creativity and ingenuity of American women. American pioneers treasured these techniques because they provided a way of reusing imported printed and colored fabrics that were too expensive (and too pretty) to be used only once. The striking patterns that were devised become even more impressive when you realize that such works arose from piles of rags. American quilters introduced another unique feature by making rows of quilting stitches that followed the contours of the patches or appliqués. Often the contours were repeated in ever-widening waves. This type of quilting is favored in Hawaii, where women have developed a style that is unique (photograph, page 1694).

Quilting Today

Quilting with a filling sandwiched between two layers of fabric originally served only a utilitarian purpose—to provide warmth. Despite today's central heating and electric blankets, few experiences are more comforting than snuggling under a cozy, handmade quilt. Two very different quilts, both suitable for snuggling, are described here (pages 1702 and 1707). An increasing number of contemporary quilters are also using old and new quilting techniques simply for the visual effects they produce. The wall hanging, opposite, and the shoulder bag, page 1694, do not need a layer of batting for insulation, but the batting puffs up around the lines of quilting, adding an interesting sculptured effect.

Modern materials allow design freedom never before possible. When quilts were frugally and painstakingly pieced together from recycled fabrics, creating a thing of beauty was a great challenge. Today, the fabric palette is almost limitless. Fabrics made of natural and synthetic fibers are available in a dazzling array of

Barbara McKie's quilted wall hanging is an example of artistic collaboration. Her husband, James, contributed the design, and Barbara provided the needlework skills needed to turn the design into a finished work. Directions for the quilted and appliquéd hanging begin on page 1697.

Barbara Barrick McKie lives in Ledyard, Connecticut with her husband, James, who provides some of the designs that Barbara's flashing needle turns into bed quilts and quilted hangings. Both are scientists whose interest in crafts and design was aroused by a visit to the Guggenheim Museum in New York. After brief forays into batiking and ceramics, Barbara took up quilting in 1971. Intrigued by quilts as decorations, she has been quilting ever since.

In pioneer days, quilting was a social craft. When a woman completed a quilt top, she would stretch it on a quilting frame and invite her neighbors to help make the quilting stitches. Conversation, dancing, eating, and games often accompanied these quilting bees.

In this detail of the album quilt, pictured at right, you can clearly read the year in which the quilt was made—1846. For such quilts, a different person made each block and then embroidered her name or signed it in indelible ink. The quilt was then assembled and quilted by one person or by all during a quilting party.

In nineteenth-century America, friends would often gather to make an album quilt such as this one for a bride-to-be, an honored member of the community, or a westward-moving neighbor.

textures and color. Synthetic batting requires less quilting to keep it from bunching up than the fillings used in the past; so it takes less time to make quilting stitches. With a sewing machine (which even hand-quilters use to seam fabric patches together) and polyester batting, making quilted items can be a joy rather than the time-consuming drudgery of yore.

Tools and Materials

Of the three layers in a quilt, it is the decorative top layer that reflects the taste and personality of the quilter. It can be made in a number of ways. Unless you are sewing a plain quilt with a single piece of fabric as a top layer (as the shoulder bag on page 1694), or you plan to do a lot of decorative quilting stitches, creating the quilt top will take the most work. Most tops are done in patchwork or appliqué, or a combination of these two. In the heyday of handmade quilts, the women making them considered their time and effort to be the least expensive ingredients. For modern quilters, these are proportionately worth much more. Using ill-suited materials wastes time and effort, since they can ruin the effect you are seeking.

Fabrics

There is nothing wrong with using scraps of fabric from previous sewing projects, if you like them and the way they look together. One way to multiply your scrap pile is to acquire scraps from friends, neighbors, and relatives. But don't use scraps salvaged from worn-out clothing if you want a long-lasting quilt. The type of fabric you choose will depend on the use to be made of the quilted object and whether you intend to launder it or have it dry-cleaned. If you combine fabrics, make sure their laundering requirements, weight, and textures are compatible. Satin does not mix well with corduroy, for example. Calico, broadcloth, chintz, gingham, percale, batiste, and cotton-and-polyester blends (the higher the percentage of cotton to polyester, the better) are usually used for quilting. But you can also use corduroy, wool, chambray, satin, velvet, duck and sailcloth if you quilt by machine or make large quilting stitches by hand. Avoid loosely woven fabrics, polyester fabrics, knits, and acrylics. Since color is not important for the quilt backing, usually an inexpensive fabric such as muslin is used. (Muslin may be used for parts of the top, too.) If you are making a bed quilt by machine, a sheet may be used for the backing. This can be a time-saver, since for most quilts you would otherwise need to piece several lengths of fabric together for the backing. If you are planning to wash your finished quilt, prewash all fabrics as a safety precaution. This will preshrink them to prevent later puckering; it will also release any dye that might run. Press the fabrics before you cut them to remove wrinkles and thus ensure accuracy.

Filler or Interlining

The filler sandwiched between the quilt top and the backing serves two purposes. It adds to the warmth of a bed quilt or quilted garment, and it imparts thickness and body, heightening the sculptural effect of the quilting stitches. In leaner times, rags, yarns, feathers, wool, grasses, even corn husks were used as fillers. When cotton batting became available, it was a great improvement, but nevertheless, it required a large amount of quilting to keep it from lumping. Many intricately designed quilting patterns were born of this necessity. Today's improved cotton batting, which comes in smooth, preshrunk blanket-sized sheets, still tends to lose its resiliency after many washings; so quilting stitches through it should leave no loose pockets larger than 3 by 3 inches. Most quilters now use polyester batting, which comes in large, seamless sheets in sizes that approximate those of blankets. This synthetic batting is light, machine-washable, and quickly dried. A good-quality polyester batt is covered on both sides with a light finish called sizing. This lets you handle the batting like fabric because its fibers will not loosen while you are working with it. Polyester batting allows greater design flexibility, since it doesn't require as much quilting as cotton batting—you can leave unquilted pockets as large as 8 by 8 inches. There are two other types of filler that are not quite substitutes for batting since they are not fluffy. Lightweight cotton blankets come in convenient sizes and are available in retail stores. They must be preshrunk before being used in a quilt that will be washed. Their main advantage is price, but since they are thin and flat, the quilt won't look as luxurious. Cotton flannel, a cotton fabric with a nap, is good to use in baby quilts, since it is very sturdy and can be washed often. It is sold in yard goods stores in widths of 36 to 45 inches.

Barbara McKie is shown at one of her favorite pastimes, sitting with her quilting hoop. The quilt she is working on is done in appliqué, with quilting stitches that follow the contours of the appliqués.

Needles

The lengths of hand-sewing needles are designated by the words *sharps* (1½ inches). and *betweens* (1¼ inches). Both sharps and betweens (No. 7, 8, 9 or 10) can be used for any quilt-making operation. Experiment to see which works better for you. Beginners usually use betweens for quilting and some manufacturers call their betweens quilting needles. Experienced quilters tend to prefer sharps for quilting. For sewing or quilting by machine, the size of the needle should be related to the weight of the fabric being sewn; in most instances, a No. 14 needle will be right.

Thread

Making a quilted item involves two stitching operations—sewing and quilting. For sewing patches together or sewing appliqués to a background fabric, use No. 50 mercerized cotton sewing thread or cotton-wrapped polyester sewing thread; the latter comes in only one weight. To quilt by hand, it is best to use special quilting thread that is silicone-treated to prevent knotting, a common occurrence in hand-stitching. It comes in white and colors. You can also use mercerized cotton or cotton-wrapped polyester sewing thread for quilting by hand or machine. But if you quilt by hand with one of these threads, draw it over a cake of beeswax to make it smoother and stiffer, thus counteracting the tendency to knot and tangle.

Frames and Hoops

If you want to hand-quilt the layers, you can put them on a quilting frame or in a quilting hoop to keep the fabric flat and wrinkle free. A quilting hoop (top, right) is available through large department stores and mail-order companies; it works on the same principle as the embroidery hoop. It consists of two concentric circles or ovals, one fitting inside the other. Both are mounted on a floor stand or a table clamp. You put the quilt, one section at a time, between the rings, and quilt from the center toward the edges. A hoop is especially handy for small articles. A quilting frame, available from mail-order companies, is more efficient for large bed quilts. This advantage can be a disadvantage, however, for a frame is uncomfortably large for the rooms in today's homes. A quilting frame is a large rectangular frame of wood, sometimes with legs. To use the frame, you cover the top and bottom crossbars with heavy fabric, stapled or thumbtacked in place. Opposite ends of the quilt are pinned to each of the crossbar fabric pieces; a turn of the clamps tightens the quilt slightly.

Hawaiian quilt designs, such as this one executed by Barbara McKie, usually suggest the luxurious plant life of the islands. The symmetrical designs are large appliqués, all cut from a single piece of fabric. The technique for cutting an appliqué resembles that used by children to make paper snowflakes; the fabric is folded into eighths, then cut into along the folds to form an eight-pointed design. The quilt is then contour-quilted with lines of stitches around each appliqué.

This large shoulder bag, 12 by 12 by 3 inches, sturdy but lightweight, was designed and made by Barbara McKie. The quilting stitches, done with thread of a color that contrasts with the fabric, produce a sharply delineated design with the three-dimensional effect characteristic of quilted work.

Hoops and frames are optional equipment. Today's quilter is more likely to want something portable to work on. The bed quilts described here accommodate this need. The quilting is done in convenient lap-sized pieces, rather than in one large unit. None of the three quilters represented here uses a quilting frame, and only one, Barbara McKie (page 1693) uses a hoop.

Miscellaneous

Dressmaker's shears, especially bent trimmers, are most efficient for cutting out many pieces of fabric from patterns. When you buy a pair, try it on for size and comfort (and if you need a left-handed pair, by all means buy it). A good pair of scissors should cut the fabric without leaving frayed edges, and blades should open and close smoothly. Reserve your best scissors for cutting only fabrics; use another pair for cutting paper and cardboard that will dull the blades. It is not necessary to own a sewing machine to make most quilted articles. However, machine sewing is faster and stronger than hand sewing. A simple straight-stitch machine can be used for all the projects in this entry except the vest (page 1706), which is appliquéd with a satin stitch obtainable only with a zigzag machine. For making and transferring patterns to fabric, you will need: pencils; a ruler or yardstick (never use a tape measure which tends to stretch and cause inaccuracies that can be disastrous in quilt making); paper; cardboard; straight pins; masking tape; a thimble (optional); and a stitch ripper for removing mistakes. For patterns, use thin, stiff poster board or cardboard, or thin plastic cut from the flat parts of containers. For marking light-colored fabrics, use a soft lead pencil; for dark fabrics, use a light-colored drawing pencil. The use of a thimble is optional; some people find one indispensable and others a nuisance.

Snow-star shoulder bag

The simple shoulder bag pictured at the left is an example of how effective quilting can be when used on a solid-color fabric. The same star design is quilted three times—on the flap, the front, and the back of the bag; the gussets, bottom, and strap have straight rows of quilting.

Materials

To make the shoulder bag you will need: ⅞ yard of 45-inch-wide cotton duck or other heavy-weight solid-color fabric (for the outside or top layer); ½ yard of 45-inch-wide unbleached muslin or other inexpensive medium-weight fabric (for the backing); ½ yard of 45-inch-wide light-weight or medium-weight solid or printed cotton or cotton-polyester fabric (for the lining); polyester quilt batting (a baby quilt size is more than enough, or use pieces left over from previous projects); a piece of tracing paper at least 6 by 6 inches; 12-by-12-inch square of crisp, heavy paper (for the perforated pattern); masking tape; pencil; yardstick or ruler; painter's powdered chalk; sandpaper; a cotton wad; scissors; sewing and quilting needles; sewing machine (optional); thread for sewing and quilting to contrast with or match the outer fabric.

Making the Pattern

By using powdered chalk with a perforated pattern, you can clearly mark a dark fabric; the chalk rubs off easily when you finish quilting. The quilting pattern, an eight-pointed star with a border, is first transferred to pattern paper. Figure A shows the entire pattern in a reduced size (opposite, top left) and a full-sized drawing of one-eighth of the pattern, which is repeated to obtain the entire design. Trace the full-sized drawing onto tracing paper, making the lines very dark. Fold the pattern paper into eighths as diagramed in Figure B; then open it and tape it to a window or a light box. Slip the one-eighth pattern section between the pattern paper and the glass, matching the dashed lines of the wedge with folds of the pattern paper. Trace over the solid pattern lines with a pencil. Remove the wedge and turn it over, pivoting along line a-b. Moving counterclockwise, insert it under the next section, again matching dashed lines with folds. Trace the pattern and

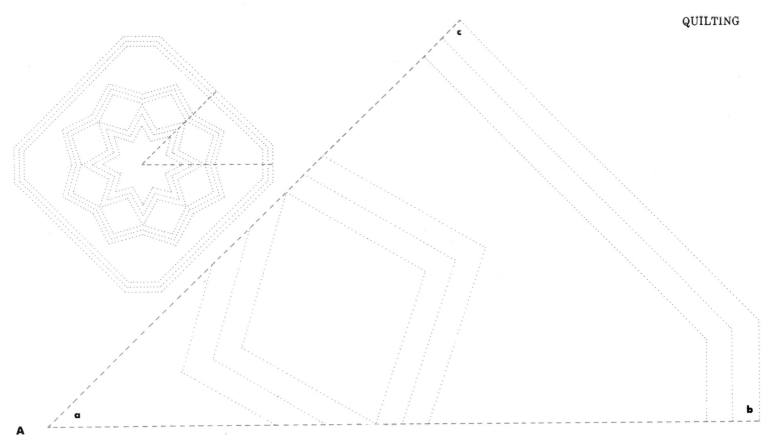

A
Figure A: The entire quilting pattern for the snow-star design is shown in reduced size (top left); the dashed line indicates the one-eighth wedge-shaped section that is drawn full size (above). Place tracing paper over the full-sized drawing and trace all the dashed and dotted lines. Mark the points a, b, and c.

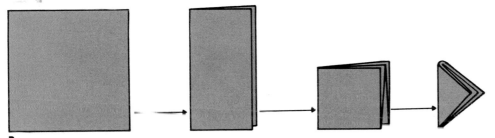

B
Figure B: Fold a 12-inch square of pattern paper into quarters, then diagonally into eighths, forming a wedge shape that corresponds to that of the one-eighth pattern section in Figure B.

remove the wedge. Turn the wedge over, pivoting along line a-c, and repeat the procedure. Continue, alternating pivot lines, until the pattern is complete. Remove the pattern and run it through an unthreaded sewing machine, perforating the solid lines. This may also be done by hand; put the pattern on a folded towel, and use a needle or straight pin to pierce holes about ⅛ inch apart along the lines. Turn the perforated pattern over, and rub the rough side gently with fine sandpaper so the holes will not close while you are using the pattern.

Making the Bag
Use a pencil and ruler to measure, mark, and cut the fabrics and batting into the pieces required. All measurements given include a ½-inch seam allowance. The layers of the front, bottom, back, and flap (the main purse section) are each cut in one piece (Figure C). From the outer fabric, cut one 13-by-40-inch main section, one 12-by-32-inch strap, and two 4-by-13-inch gusset pieces. From both the lining and backing fabrics, cut one 13-by-40-inch main section and two 4-by-13-inch gusset pieces. Since batting is harder to mark than fabric, pin the cut backing pieces to the batting and use them as patterns as you cut one main section and two gusset pieces. Also mark and cut one 3-by-32-inch piece of batting for the strap. With pencil and ruler, mark the dashed lines and dots of Figure C on the backing fabric and on the wrong side of the lining fabric.

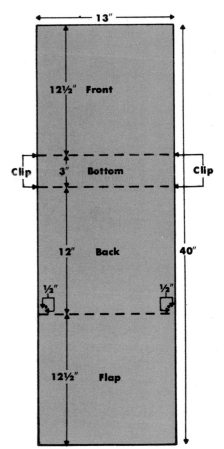

C
Figure C: Follow this diagram of the main purse section when you mark the backing and lining fabrics. The dashed lines indicate folds; the dots mark where the seams will end.

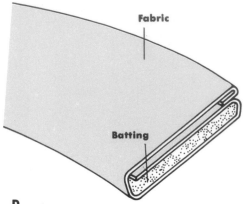

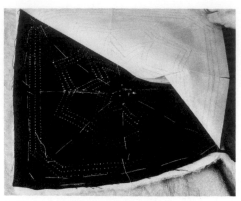

Figure D: To make the shoulder-bag strap, wrap the outer fabric around the batting strip, as shown in this cross-section diagram. What will be the underside of the strap has two layers of the outer fabric, one with an edge turned under ¼ inch. Quilting stitches will hold the sandwich together.

1: To transfer the perforated pattern to fabric, rub powdered chalk gently through the perforations, using a wad of cotton.

2: If you handle the fabric carefully, the chalk should not dust off accidentally during quilting. But if it does, you can always repeat the process.

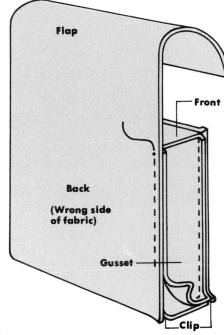

Figure E: Right sides facing (the bag is inside out), sew the side gussets to the main purse section, making ½-inch-wide seams. Before stitching, clip ⅜ inch into the seam allowance for the main section. (See also Figure C, page 1695).

Basting: When all the pieces have been cut and marked, baste the corresponding backing, batting, and outer fabric pieces together. (The lining is attached after the quilting is done.) To baste the main section together, place the outer fabric, face down, on a flat surface, place the batting on it; then place the backing (marked side up) on top of the batting. Pin the three layers together, making sure edges are even. Then baste them together along the dashed lines, diagonally from corner to corner across each section, and around the outside edges. Pin each of the two sets of three gusset pieces together; baste around the outside edges. To assemble the shoulder strap, encase the batting in the outer fabric piece as shown in Figure D. Pin the layers together, and baste around the outside edges.

Transferring the quilting pattern: Pin the perforated pattern to the outside-fabric flap section, leaving a ½-inch seam allowance at the sides and ends of the flap. Transfer the pattern to the fabric (photograph 1), using powdered chalk and a wad of cotton. This will make lines of dots (photograph 2). After you quilt the flap, you will repeat the pattern transfer process on the front and quilt it, then on the back and quilt it.

Quilting the shoulder bag: The Craftnotes on page 1701 tell how to quilt by hand or by machine. Quilt the star design and borders on the flap, front, and back, following the chalked lines in sequence. To quilt the gusset pieces, make 11 parallel rows of stitches along the longest dimension. Place the first row ¼ inch in from the seam line, and space subsequent rows ¼ inch apart. Quilt the bottom as you did the gussets, placing the first row on the marked fold line. Quilt the shoulder strap the same way, but omit the three center rows.

Assembling the bag: To assemble the quilted fabric pieces, first pin the gussets to the main section, right sides facing so the bag is inside out, as shown in Figure E. While you are pinning, clip into the seam allowance of the main section about ⅜ inch at the points indicated in both Figures E and C (page 1695). This clipping should match points ½ inch from the corners of the gusset pieces; it allows the fabric to turn and lie properly. Sew the gussets to the front, bottom, and back of the main section; make ½-inch seams, pivoting at the bottom just inside the clip. End the stitching at the dot marked in Figure E and Figure C. This leaves the top ½ inch of the gusset free. Turn the bag right side out and set it aside.

Assemble the lining pieces in the same manner as you assembled the quilted bag, again with right sides facing. However, gradually increase the seam allowance to ¾ inch when you reach the bottom and make the clips (indicated by the dots) ⅝ inch deep. This is to make sure that the lining will fit inside the bag without bunching. Leave the assembled lining inside out.

Press the raw edges of the outer bag ½ inch to the inside; press the raw edges of the lining to the outside. Wrong sides facing, place the lining inside the outer bag. Pin together all around; leave the flap for last, and adjust any excess lining there. Insert the strap ends ½ inch deep between the lining and the outer bag gussets. Then stitch the lining to the outer bag, sewing ⅛ inch in from the turned-under edges. Double- or triple-stitch along the top edges of the gussets to reinforce the joining points.

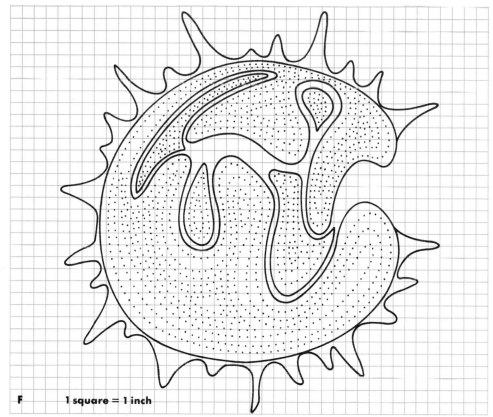

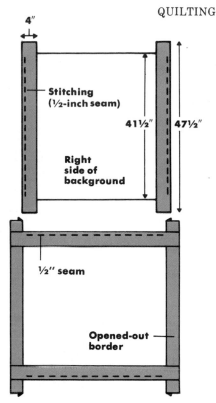

Figure F: To make a full-sized pattern for the quilted hanging, draw a 1-inch grid on plain paper. Square by square, copy the pattern onto the larger grid. The solid lines of the pattern are the cutting lines; include the dotted lines as a quilting guide if you wish to mark them rather than quilting freehand.

Figure G: Pin the lengthwise borders to the background fabric, right sides facing, with raw edges even and centers matched. Stitch together with ½-inch seams, beginning and ending ½ inch in from the side edges of the background fabric (top). Open out the lengthwise border strips and pin the crosswise borders to the background fabric, right sides facing, again matching the centers and raw edges. Sew the crosswise borders only to the background fabric (not to the lengthwise borders), making ½-inch seams (bottom). Open out the crosswise borders.

Needlecrafts

Organic wall hanging

$ 🗙 🚶 🧵

The unusual design of the 42-by-45½-inch wall hanging pictured on page 1690 was inspired by the shapes of microscopic creatures such as amoebae and paramecia. This type of quilting, called contour quilting, was done by hand in concentric rows that parallel the outlines of the green and turquoise appliqués.

Materials

The fabrics used for this hanging are medium-weight cotton or cotton-and-polyester blends. You will need the following amounts of 45-inch-wide fabric: 2⅜ yards of purple; 2½ yards of ivory; ¾ yard of green; and ⅜ yard of turquoise. In addition, you will need: one piece of polyester batting measuring at least 42 by 46½ inches; a 36-by-36-inch square of thin, stiff paper (for enlarging the pattern); pencil; ruler or yardstick; scissors; sewing and quilting needles; sewing machine (optional); straight pins; sewing thread; and quilting thread in black and white. The quilting may be done freehand, without marking any guidelines on the fabric. If you prefer to follow marked lines when quilting, you will need the following materials to transfer the pattern: light-colored painter's chalk, fine sandpaper, and a wad of cotton. To hang the finished piece, you will need a wooden dowel 1 inch in diameter and at least 42 inches long.

First Steps

Prepare the patterns: Enlarge the pattern for the appliqué pieces (Figure F). If you would like to have quilting lines on the fabric rather than quilting freehand, add them to the enlarged pattern, using a pencil of a different color to distinguish them from the cutting lines. Cut the pattern into pieces along the cutting lines so you have one pattern piece for the purple fabric, one for the green, and four for the turquoise. If you have transferred the quilting lines, perforate the pattern by machine-stitching along these lines with an unthreaded machine or pierce holes ⅛ inch apart with a straight pin or needle. Turn the perforated pattern over and smooth the perforations lightly with sandpaper to keep them from closing later.

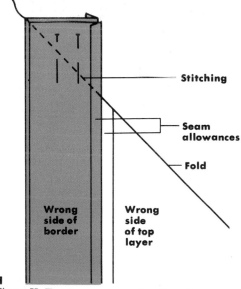

Figure H: To miter a corner, place the adjacent border edges together, right sides facing. (This will make a diagonal fold in the background fabric.) Secure the strips with pins; then stitch them together, as shown, at a 45-degree angle.

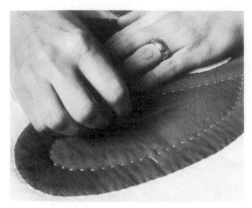

3: To make a temporary guideline to follow when you do freehand contour quilting, make an indentation in the fabric with the needle point.

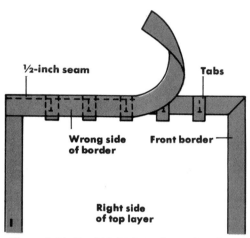

Figure I: Pin the folded tabs to the top front border, spacing them evenly, with the middle tab at the center. Pin the back border strips to the corresponding front border strips, right sides facing, sandwiching the tabs between along the top. Sew together on all outer edges, making ½-inch seams and catching the tabs in the top seam.

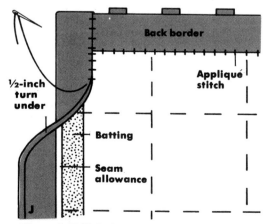

Figure J: Fold the back borders to the back, turn the unstitched raw edges under ½ inch, and press. Then sew the folded edges to the backing fabric.

Cut the fabric: Pin the individual pattern pieces to fabric of the right color, with grid lines parallel to the grain (lengthwise and crosswise threads) of the fabric. Cut out the appliqués ¼ inch outside the edge of the patterns to provide a turn-under allowance. In addition to the appliqués, cut the following: from the ivory fabric, cut two 37-by-41½-inch pieces (for the background and the backing); from the purple fabric, cut four 4-by-47½-inch strips, four 4-by-43-inch strips (for the borders), and one 3-by-45-inch strip (for the hanging tabs).

Appliquéing
Start by pinning the green appliqué to the center of the background fabric. Next pin the adjacent purple piece in place, extending it under the green edge by ½ inch to allow for the ¼ inch of green that will be turned under. (The outer edge of the green piece is appliquéd on top of the inner edge of the purple piece, which is not sewn separately.) Finally, pin the turquoise pieces in place. Baste all pieces carefully ½ to ¾ inch in from the raw edges. Make sure each piece lies smooth and flat. Following the directions in the Craftnotes on page 1700, appliqué the pieces in this order: first the outer purple edge, then the outer green edge over the raw inner purple edge, then the inner green edges, and finally the turquoise edges.

Assembling and Quilting
Assemble the top layer first. Measure and mark the center points of two long border strips, two short border strips, and the edges of the background fabric. Right sides facing, stitch these borders to the background fabric (Figure G, page 1697). To miter the corners where the borders meet, fold the background fabric diagonally at the corner, matching the unstitched ends of adjacent border strips. Stitch together diagonally as shown in Figure H, page 1697. Repeat the procedure on the three remaining corners. The top layer is now completely assembled.

Put the top layer, right side down, on a flat surface and tape it there to keep it from shifting. Place the piece of batting on top of the taped-down fabric; pin batting and fabric together around the edges, keeping the batting as smooth as possible. Remove the tape and carefully trim the batting to the same size as the top layer. Place the backing piece of fabric on top of the batting, with an equal margin of batting extending all around. Baste all three layers together, beginning at the center and stitching outward in a sunburst pattern (page 1701). Remove all pins.

The next step is quilting. If you wish, transfer the quilting lines to the fabric pieces using painter's chalk and a wad of cotton (photographs 1 and 2, page 1696). Use white thread to quilt around the outside of all appliqués, as close to the turned-under edge as possible. If you have marked them, quilt subsequent rows following the dotted lines. (White thread is used for the turquoise appliqués, black thread for the green.) If you have decided to do the quilting freehand, work each subsequent row within each appliqué as an echo of the shape of the outside edge. Keep the rows smoothly curved; as a guide, score the fabric an inch or two ahead with the point of the needle (photograph 3). Complete stitching each row before going on to the next. Most rows should be about ½ inch apart, but you can vary the spacing from ¼ to 1 inch in order to accommodate the narrower and wider areas of the appliqués.

Finishing
To make the hanging tabs, fold the 3-by-45-inch strip of fabric in half lengthwise, right side inside. Stitch along the lengthwise edge, making a ¼-inch seam. Turn the strip right side out, and press it with an iron so the seam lies along one edge. Cut the strip into five 9-inch tabs.

Place the quilted hanging, right side up, on a flat surface. Fold the tabs in half crosswise, and spacing them evenly, pin them across the top of the hanging, raw edges even with the top edge of the border. Right sides facing, pin the four remaining border strips to the four front borders, raw edges matching. Sew each strip in place with a ½-inch seam (Figure I). Turn the back border strips to the back, pressing under ½-inch seam allowances as shown in Figure J. (It is not necessary to miter the corners on the back.) With tiny stitches, sew the folded-under edges to the back of the hanging by hand. Remove the pins and basting stitches. Slip a dowel through the tabs, and use two nails to suspend the hanging from the wall.

CRAFTNOTES: TRADITIONAL QUILTING PATTERNS

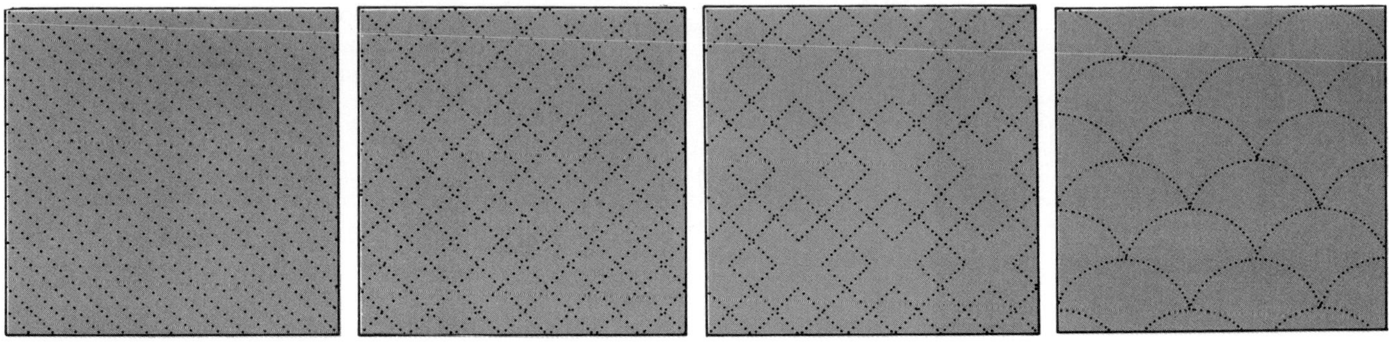

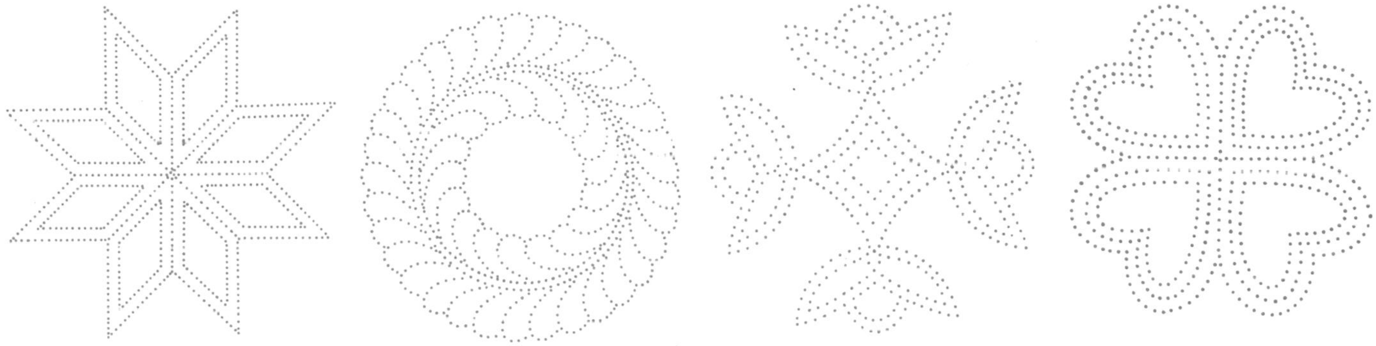

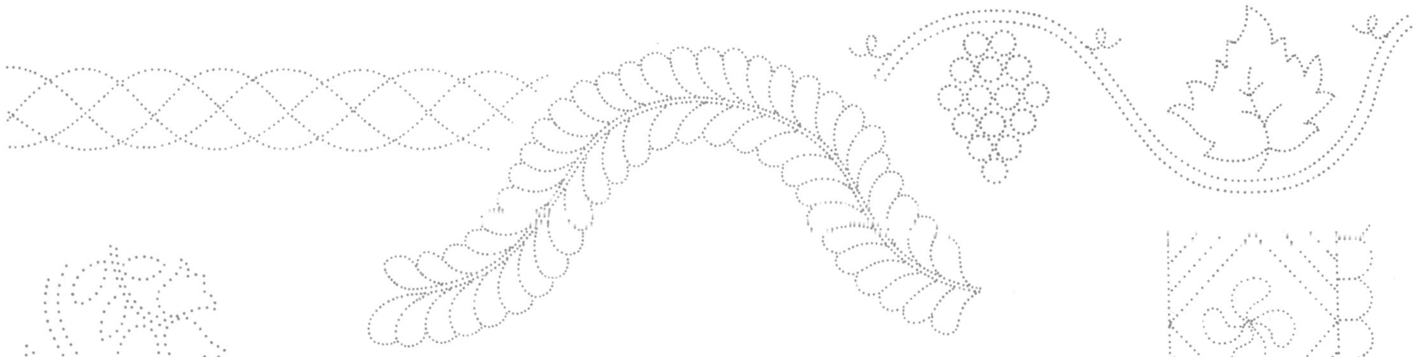

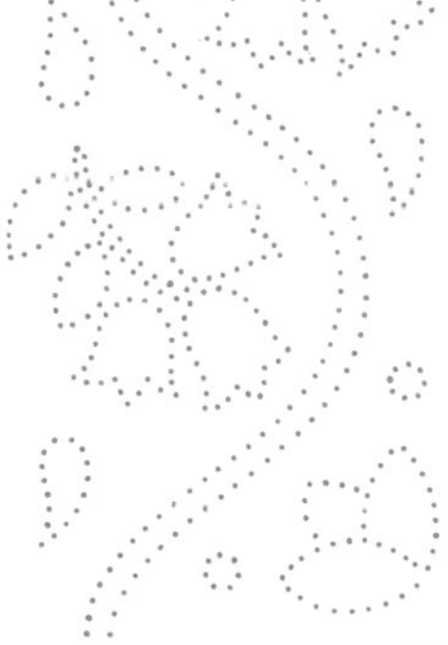

The treasury of traditional quilting patterns, some of which are shown here, is virtually limitless. But all patterns are basically a series of curved or straight lines, and even the most elaborate design can be copied with the aid of a ruler and a compass or curved objects you can trace, such as cups, saucers, or jar lids. The selection and arrangement of a pattern hinge on the quilter's skill and taste, the time available, and the shape of the fabric patches or appliques in the quilt top. Although the traditional patterns for quilting stitches have always served the practical purpose of holding the layers together, they have come to be used as a decorative element as well.

Patchwork

Patchwork, the method of sewing small patches of fabric together to form a larger piece, is a technique in which accuracy plays an important part. The fabric patches—and the patterns, or templates, from which they are cut—must be marked and cut carefully so they will fit together with precision. In addition, as many pattern edges as possible should be placed along the straight grain (lengthwise and crosswise threads) of the fabric. Patches cut on the bias tend to stretch and should be avoided. Cut patterns for patchwork from thin, stiff cardboard because you will trace them several times. If you will be cutting a large number of fabric patches of one shape, make several identical patterns. Discard worn patterns when their edges become frayed from frequent tracings. Durable patterns for small shapes can be cut from thin plastic (use the flat parts of containers).

Marking, cutting, and machine stitching:

Make sure that all patterns have a uniform seam allowance added on all sides and that your pencil point and scissors are sharp. Many quilters insist that patches should be marked and cut individually to ensure accuracy. To mark an individual patch, place the pattern on the wrong side of the fabric, and trace around it with a pencil. Use a dark pencil for light-colored fabrics, a light-colored pencil (not chalk—the line it makes is too wide) for dark fabrics. Carefully cut out the patch, following the marked line. Other quilters maintain that cutting patches individually is unnecessary, except when you are working with heavy fabrics such as corduroy or velvet. As a time-saver and to add stability to lighter weight fabrics, you can cut several patches of the same shape at one time. Triple or quadruple the fabric and pin or baste the layers together temporarily. Then trace the pattern on the top layer only, and cut all layers simultaneously. Try both methods with different fabrics, and use the one that works better for you.

When you sew the patches, pin or baste them together, right sides facing. Make sure the raw edges of the sides to be seamed are even. Stitch the seam, using the markings on your sewing machine's needle plate or the edge of the presser foot to maintain a uniform seam allowance. After each patchwork unit is sewn together, press the seams to one side (open seams weaken the construction). If you are combining light and dark fabric, press the seam to the desk side so it will not show through.

Marking, cutting, and hand stitching:

Since so many seams are involved, most people use a sewing machine to do patchwork. If you sew by hand, the procedures are generally the same except that you do not have a needle plate or presser foot to measure the seam allowance. Therefore, make patterns actual size, without a seam allowance. When you trace the pattern on the fabric, you will mark the seam line instead of the cutting line. Cut out the patch outside this seam line, with a seam allowance around. When you sew the patches together, match up the marked seam line.

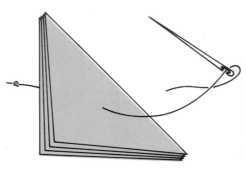

Handling quantities of patches: Once they are cut, a good way to keep a large number of patches orderly is to group them according to shape and color. Then string each group together by running a thread, knotted at one end, through the centers (above). Lift off each piece as it is needed.

Appliqué

An appliqué is a piece of fabric that is sewn onto a larger piece of background fabric. Appliqués sewn on by hand have narrow turned-under edges; so they should be cut on the bias (cross grain) of the fabric to make it easier to turn under any curved edges.

Right side up, pin the appliqué to the right side of the background fabric, smoothing it down as you pin. Then baste all around, ½ to ¾ inch in from the raw edges.

Begin with a knot at the end of the thread. Using the tip of the needle as a tool, smoothly turn the raw edge of the appliqué under 3/16 to ¼ inch (top right). With the needle, smooth and crease the turned-under edge (middle right). All-cotton fabric creases the best.

Hold the turned-under edge with your thumb just ahead of where you will be stitching. The stitch used to appliqué is a tiny, almost invisible stitch. To begin, bring the needle and thread through to the right side of the fabric, catching a few threads of the appliqué in the process. Then insert the needle into the background fabric and bring it up at an angle, ⅛ inch away or less from the last stitch (bottom right). On the right side the visible stitches are tiny and perpendicular to the edge of the appliqué. On the wrong side they are larger and diagonal.

Sharp inside and outside corners are a challenge, and it takes practice to make them neatly.

For inside corners (or concave curves), turn the edge under using the tip of the needle as usual, but run the needle around the corner several times to get the edge to stay under. Hold the turned-under edge with your thumb a bit closer to the stitches than usual. Then take several small appliqué stitches close together to keep the raw edge from popping out.

For sharp outside corners, stitch as usual to within ⅛ inch of the point of the corner. Then take two stitches in the same place at the point. Push under the raw edge of the adjacent side, with the needle tip, and make the next stitch ⅛ inch away or less.

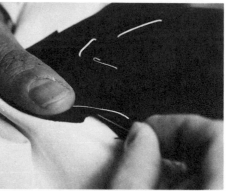

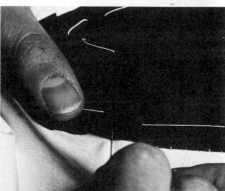

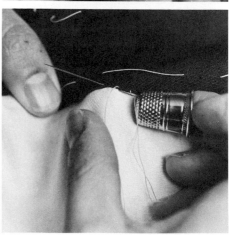

PATCHWORK, APPLIQUÉ, AND QUILTING

Quilting

Basting: Before you begin to quilt either by hand or machine, you should baste together the top, batting, and bottom layers so they do not shift during the quilting process. Make sure both bottom and top fabric layers have been prewashed and pressed.

Put the quilt backing, wrong side up, on a flat surface. Place the batting on top of the backing; then smooth the top layer in place. The photograph above shows these three layers. Pin the three layers together.

Next, baste the layers together with rows of long basting stitches. Begin each row at the center of the quilt, and stitch out to the corners and sides, making a sunburst pattern (above). Then baste around the edges. As you baste, smooth the layers and check frequently to make sure the stitches penetrate all three layers.

Quilting by hand: The quilting stitch is a running stitch—small, straight stitches in a row. You should make between five and twelve stitches per inch; the number will vary from person to person and according to the thickness of the quilt. Regardless of size, it is important that the stitches be of even length. Always start in the center of the section being worked on, and take several stitches before pulling the needle and thread through.

To quilt by hand, thread a quilting needle with a single 15-inch-long strand of quilting thread or sewing thread that has been pulled over a cake of beeswax. Gather the three-layered sandwich in your non-stitching hand, or, if you are using a frame or hoop, place your free hand beneath it.

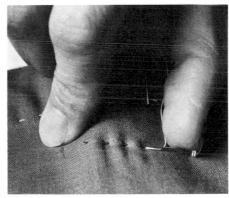

To begin, insert the needle in the quilt top and batting about 1 inch from where you plan to make the first stitch. Bring the needle up where the first stitch will start, leaving a short tail of thread on the surface. From underneath, put your index finger against the line to be quilted. You can protect the finger from the needle point with adhesive tape. Make several running stitches in the direction opposite to the one in which you will be quilting, penetrating all three layers (above).

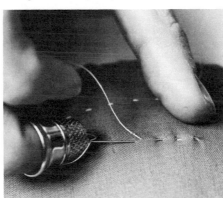

Then double back, making stitches in the right direction in exactly the same places as the first series was made (above). Having thus an-

chored the thread, snip off the tail close to the surface and continue stitching. When you reach the end of the thread or the end of the row, anchor the thread again the same way.

Another way to begin and end a length of thread is with a knot. When you begin a row, make a small knot at the end of the thread. Insert the needle from the back, and give the thread a tug from the front, forcing the knot through the bottom layer and embedding it in the batting. To end the thread, quilt to within one stitch of the end of the row; then make a small knot in the thread, close to the surface. Make the last stitch, and ,penetrating only the top layer and part of the batting, bring the needle up about an inch from the last stitch. Give the thread a tug, burying the knot in the batting; then cut the thread off close to the surface of the quilt.

Quilting by machine: If you quilt by machine, you will do so at home; so the portability of the project is reduced. In addition, many people find it hard to sew a smooth curve; even mass-produced quilts made by experienced sewers often have uneven curves. But if you do block-by-block quilting (page 1703), the smaller units are more maneuverable than a whole quilt.

To quilt by machine, set the stitch length at 6 to 10 stitches per inch and use a No. 14 needle. Practice quilting on a test block of the same batting and fabrics that will be used in the quilt. Follow your sewing-machine manual in making adjustments in the stitch length, the thread tension, or the pressure on the presser foot, so the quilting thread will go smoothly and evenly through the thickness of the quilt. For straight-line quilting, you will find a quilting foot helpful. This attachment acts as a guide in spacing parallel rows of quilting stitches.

When you begin to quilt, start at the center and quilt outward, as in hand quilting. Always start with a full bobbin so you do not run out of thread in the middle of a row. When the quilting is finished, pull all of the ends of top thread to the back and knot them with bobbin thread ends. Trim the ends close to the knot.

Gladys Boalt's love for quilts began when her mother gave her a book about quilting. Her first quilt took her eight years to complete, but after she discovered block-by-block quilting, she became engrossed in the craft. Ms. Boalt, who studied illustration and advertising at Pratt Institute, exhibits her work at fairs, schools, and libraries, and makes quilted pillows and hangings for the Gazebo, a crafts boutique. She conducts once-a-week quilting bees at her home in Stormville, New York, and teaches quilting at nearby art centers.

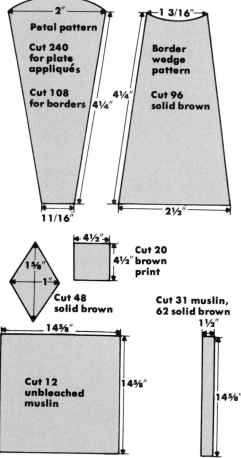

Petal pattern
2"
Cut 240 for plate appliqués
4¼" 4¼"
Cut 108 for borders

Border wedge pattern
1 3/16"
4¼"
Cut 96 solid brown

11/16" 2½"

1⅝" 1"
4½"
4½"
Cut 20 brown print

Cut 48 solid brown

Cut 31 muslin, 62 solid brown
1½"

14⅝"

Cut 12 unbleached muslin
14⅝" 14⅝"

14⅝"

K
Figure K: Follow these measurements as you use a pencil and ruler to draw these pattern outlines on cardboard. But before cutting, add a 3/16-inch seam allowance on all sides.

A quilt with an Early American flavor decorates the bed of a colonial-style bedroom. Traditional patterns such as this Dresden-plate design add a note of warmth and coziness. Gladys Boalt made this 66-by-85-inch quilt to fit a three-quarter-sized bed, but you can adapt the design to fit a bed of any size.

Needlecrafts
Dresden-plate quilt

The design for the Dresden-plate quilt pictured above, also known as the aster or the friendship ring, combines quilting with patchwork and appliqué to form the quilt top. Most antique Dresden-plate quilts are worked in pastel colors, but the design fits a modern decor when bright or dark-and-light colors are used. The pattern was popular in colonial times when women traded fabric scraps. An old Dresden-plate quilt might include 500 to 1,000 different fabric prints, with no two petals alike. For your quilt, you might choose, say, 20 prints, a different one for each of the 20 petals in each plate, or you might prefer to alternate fewer fabrics.

The 66-by-85-inch bedspread-type quilt shown here fits a three-quarter-sized bed and is made from 12 appliquéd squares joined with decorative strips and edged with a scalloped border. To adapt the design for beds of other sizes, add or subtract squares or strips as necessary. On page 1707 are directions for measuring a bed. With these measurements in hand, juggle the number of squares and strips until you hit upon the combination that will give you the size you need. Each appliquéd block, after seaming, is approximately 14½ inches square. Finished, each set of three joining strips is approximately 4½ inches wide. The finished width of the border is 4 inches. But in determining how many strips and blocks you need to fit your bed, you must allow for a 1-inch shrinkage of each block during the quilting process; that is, it will end up being 13½ inches square. The strips too will shrink, but only slightly. By omitting the joining strips and corner squares, sewing together 24 squares in four rows of six, and then adding the scalloped border, a 62-by-89-inch bedspread, to fit a twin-sized bed, could be made. A coverlet to fit a full-sized bed would require 25 squares arranged in five rows of five, plus connecting strips, corner squares, and a border. Work out the combination on paper, and refer to the sketch later to determine the number of pieces to cut from each fabric. Adjust the amounts of fabric and batting needed, and adapt the directions that follow to conform to the measurements you need.

Materials

To make the quilt in the size shown you will need the following amounts of 45-inch-wide cotton or cotton-and-polyester fabric: 6 yards of unbleached muslin (for appliquéd squares and joining strips); 3 yards—you may use scraps from previous projects—of assorted brown prints (for plate petals and border); ½ yard of dark brown calico print (for corner squares); 2 yards of solid dark brown (for strips and border); 6 yards of a lightweight cotton fabric, such as batiste, in a small print (for the backing). You will also need a roll of double-bed-sized polyester quilt batting; tracing paper; pencil; ruler; carbon paper; scissors; thin, stiff cardboard (for patterns); straight pins; iron; quilting and sewing needles; quilting and sewing thread, or sewing thread and a cake of beeswax. For the binding, you need 10 yards of 1-inch-wide bias tape (or you can make your own from ¾ yard of fabric—see page 1704).

Block-by-Block Quilting

Although making a quilt may seem a formidable task, this particular pattern is quite easy to do. With a block-by-block quilting technique, an entire block can be assembled and quilted in a single evening.

The Dresden-plate design is formed by sewing petals together into a plate shape, then appliquéing the plate onto a plain square. Edging strips are sewn onto the appliquéd square; then batting and backing fabric are added, so each block is a tiny quilt. These are quilted separately, then joined by stitching the front layers of the blocks together by machine. The edges of the backs of the blocks are then turned under and stitched by hand. In the days when it was the practice to spread out a whole quilt or put it in a frame, blocks were sewn together to form a single large top layer. Then batting and backing fabric of the same size were added, and the quilting was done on one large piece. Block-by-block quilting is more convenient. It makes hoops and frames unnecessary, since each block can be held easily. This makes the project portable. Also, when a curved line is being quilted, the small block can be shifted around so you are always working in a comfortable direction (usually toward you).

Making the Blocks

Using the dimensions in Figure K, measure and draw the patterns directly on cardboard. Then add a 3/16-inch seam allowance on each side. Cut out the patterns along the outer lines. Edges will become worn from repeated tracings; so make several patterns of the petal, diamond, and border pieces—those that will be traced most frequently.

Figure K also gives the number of pieces of fabric to cut in each color. For how to mark and cut the pieces, refer to the Craftnotes on page 1700.

When all the pieces have been cut, you are ready to begin sewing them together to form the 12 blocks. Unless otherwise indicated, all pieces are sewn together with right sides facing, making 3/16-inch seams. Press all seams to one side after each step; pressing seams open weakens the construction. For each block, make one plate by stitching 20 petal-shaped pieces together along their long sides, forming a ring. When the plate is completed, press all the seams to one side and then center the plate on a 15-inch muslin square. To center the plate appliqué, fold the square into quarters and lightly crease the folds at the center. Unfold the square and use the creases as a guide in placing the plate. Pin the appliqué, right side up, to the square; insert a pin through each petal and smooth the fabric as you pin. Following the Craftnotes on page 1700, sew the appliqué onto the muslin square using appliqué stitches. Turn under the 3/16-inch seam allowance, and sew first around the inner and then the outer edges of the appliqué.

After the plate design has been appliquéd, pin four diamonds to the center of the plate, again using the creases as a guide. Then appliqué the diamonds to the muslin as you did the plates.

The feather-edged star design that Gladys Boalt used for a pillow dates back to the early 1800's and is considered one of the most difficult patterns, combining patchwork, appliqué, and quilting.

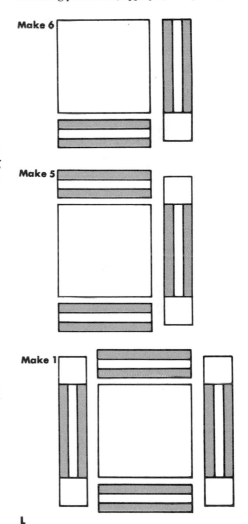

Make 6

Make 5

Make 1

L

Figure L: To make the twelve blocks required, sew the plain strip units to the small muslin squares first, in the positions indicated. Press the seams to one side; then add the strip-and-square units, following the diagrams to obtain the required number of each type of block.

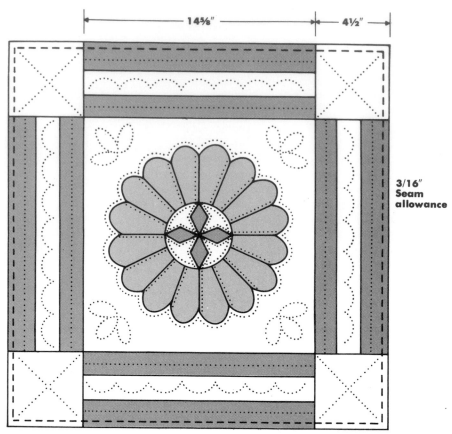

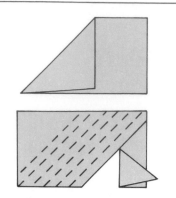

Bias strips

Bias strips of fabric, cut at a 45-degree angle across the grain of the fabric, have more stretch and give than strips cut on the straight grain; they are used to bind and finish the raw edges of a quilt. They are also used to make piping. You can purchase bias tape in widths from ½ to 1½ inches, and in solid colors as well as some prints. But for a perfect match and a custom look, make your own bias tape by piecing together strips of fabric that you have cut.

To make bias tape, fold one corner of a rectangle or square of fabric on the bias (above, top). Crease the fold.

Using the crease as a guide, mark the fabric with parallel lines the desired width of the bias strips. Cut along the marked lines (above).

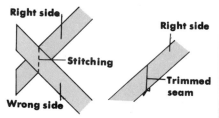

To sew the strips together to form one long strip of the required length, place the ends together, right sides facing (above, left). Then stitch along the straight grain.

When the strips are opened up, the seam will appear diagonal (above, right). Trim the seam to about ¼ inch and press it open to avoid extra bulk.

M

Figure M: For each block, quilt around the appliqués and patches as close to the seams as you can. When quilting the Xs in the corner squares, stop stitching ½ inch in from the edges so the seam allowance is left open; the last few quilting stitches can be made after seaming.

The next step is to add the joining strips and corner squares to the appliquéd muslin squares. It may seem logical to sew the strips to the sides of the muslin squares and then add the corner squares. However, this forces you to sew the corner squares into the 90-degree angle formed by the joining strips. To do this, you have to make a sharp turn exactly at the point where the seams of the strips meet—a tedious operation if you do it for all 20 corner squares, especially if you are using a sewing machine. To eliminate this, first sew the joining strips together in units of three, with one muslin strip between the brown ones. Then sew corner squares to one or both ends of some of the units. If you are making a 12-block quilt, you will have 31 strip assemblies; sew a corner square onto one end of six of these and onto both ends of seven. Finally, sew the strip units and then the strip-and-square units onto the muslin square as shown in Figure L on page 1703. If you are making a quilt that is not the size shown, use Figures L and N as guides as you calculate how many strip units and strip-and-square units you will need to make the number of blocks required. (Additional blocks for larger quilts are made by repeating those in the middle vertical and horizontal rows in Figure N.)

Quilting the Blocks

Place a finished block, face down, on a flat surface. Cut a piece of batting the size of the block and place it on top. Then cut a piece of backing fabric 1 inch larger than the block on each side. (For example, if you have a 19-inch square block, make the backing 21 inches square.) Pin and baste the three layers together, smoothing out any wrinkles. Use Figure M as a guide in determining where to place the lines of quilting; draw the leaves and scallops on the fabric with a pencil. The other lines may also be drawn, but if you use the seam lines as a guide, they can easily be quilted freehand. Refer to the Craftnotes on page 1701 for quilting directions, and quilt each block, working your way out from the center toward the edges. Do not quilt into the seam allowance. When all the blocks have been quilted, sew them together (Figure N) by seaming the front layers only. To prevent the batting and backing layers from catching in the seam, pin them out of the way. Place the blocks to be seamed together, right sides facing, and sew with a 3/16-inch seam.

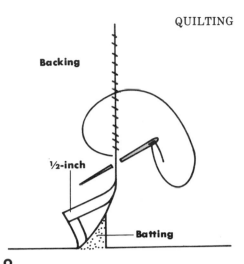

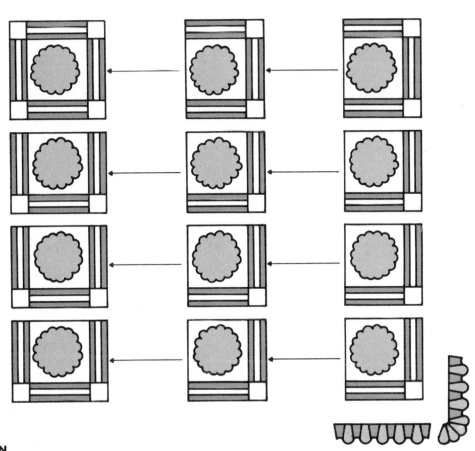

O

Figure O: Since each block was quilted separately, you will need to finish the backing seams between blocks. Overlap adjacent backing edges, folding the top edge under ½ inch. Sew with a tiny hem stitch as shown, catching only the underlayer of backing, not the filling.

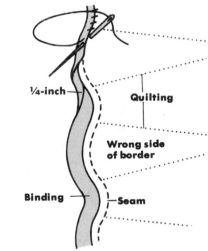

P

Figure P: To finish the outer edges of the quilt, sew bias tape to the right side of the border edge, right sides facing. Then turn the tape to the back and fold the raw tape edge under ¼ inch. Sew the tape down by hand with small stitches.

N

Figure N: To put the quilted blocks together, first sew them into vertical rows of four; then sew these three vertical rows together. When you have made and quilted the four border strips, sew on the top and bottom strips first; then add the side strips.

The Border

The border is assembled in four strips, for the top, the bottom, and each side. First, the front of each strip is pieced together, then batting and backing are added. The strips are then quilted and sewn in place as were the blocks. For the front of the top and bottom border strips, sew 20 print-fabric petals together, alternating with 21 of the solid-color border petals. The top layer of each side border strip is made with 26 print petals alternating with 27 solid petals. To each end of each side border strip, add four print petals whose narrow ends have been trimmed to a width of ⅜ inch (Figure N). This forms a fan-shaped curved corner.

Pin and baste the batting and backing to each border strip as for the blocks. Then quilt each strip close to the seams of each petal (remember to quilt only to within ½ inch of the raw edges to allow for seams; put in the last few stitches after the quilt has been assembled).

Again referring to Figure N, stitch the fronts of the border strips to the block fronts, pinning the batting and lining back out of the way.

Finishing

To finish the backing, trim away excess batting so adjacent edges fit together smoothly. Overlap the edges of the backing, turning the top edge under ½ inch; hand sew the folded edge down, forming a felled seam (Figure O). Finish all edges in this way except the outside one, which is finished with a binding.

For the binding, purchase 1-inch-wide bias tape or make your own following the directions opposite. (Approximately 10 yards of tape were needed to finish the edges of the quilt shown.) Right sides facing, pin the bias tape around the scalloped perimeter of the quilt, raw edges even. Overlap the ends where they meet, turning the edge of the top end under ¼ inch. Sew the tape to the quilt, making a 3/16- to ¼-inch seam. Then fold the tape to the wrong side of the quilt (Figure P) and hand-sew the edge to the quilt back, thus encasing the raw edges of the quilt.

Karen Katz is a fabric artist who creates clothes, quilts, and quilted tapestries for individuals and for commercial reproduction. For Ms. Katz, who directs the crafts department at Marymount College in New York, creating a design and watching it develop is an exciting experience. The projects here show she has a love for luxurious fabrics, rich color, and fanciful subject matter.

Needlecrafts
Cloudy-day vest and skirt $ ☒ ⚹ ♨

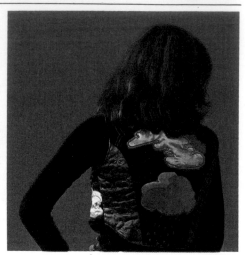

Karen Katz used one of her favorite materials—satin—to add clouds and raindrops to an ordinary pattern, giving this vest flash and originality. A matching skirt with a cloud pocket completes the outfit.

For the outfit pictured, colors both vivid and pastel were used to make satin clouds that were then machine-appliquéd to a satin vest and skirt made from a purchased dressmaker's pattern. The raveled edges that are so often visible in machine-stitched appliqués can be eliminated with the glue technique described here.

Materials
To make the vest, purchase a pattern for a simple lined vest. Referring to the pattern envelope for the amounts of fabric needed, use black satin for the outside fabric; prequilted fabric for the filling (you will need the same amount as you did of the outer fabric; prequilting eliminates the need of a backing fabric); and lining fabric such as taffeta or satin. Prequilted fabric can also be used in side insets if the pattern calls for them, as in the vest pictured. For the appliqués you will need small amounts of satin in various colors that will contrast with the background fabric. Additional tools and materials needed are: a zigzag sewing machine; sewing thread in several colors similar to, but not necessarily the same as, the appliqués; paper; pencil; ruler; scissors; straight pins; sewing needle; white glue; a dish for mixing the glue with water; a small pointed paintbrush; and tailor's chalk.

Making the Vest
Following the pattern directions, cut the outer fabric, the prequilted fabric, and the lining pieces. Cut the prequilted pieces from the outer fabric pattern pieces and eliminate any interfacing. Pin the outside pieces to the corresponding prequilted pieces, wrong sides facing. Baste each section together and set aside.

Enlarge the cloud designs (Figure Q), or draw your own. Cut out the patterns, and with a light colored pencil, transfer the outlines to the wrong side of the satin fabric. Then use this technique to keep edges from raveling after they are cut. Mix one part of water with three parts of white glue. Apply the diluted glue in ⅛-inch-wide lines inside the marked edges of the appliqués, letting the glue extend just over the lines. Let the glue dry thoroughly; then cut out the appliqués. The glue will hold the cut fabric threads in place.

Pin the cloud appliqués to the outer vest pieces. Arrange them as you like, singly or overlapping in groups. When you are satisfied with the design, baste the pieces in place. Set the sewing machine to a zigzag satin stitch, wide enough to cover the glued edge of the appliqués. Sew all around the edge of each cloud, through the outer fabric and the prequilted batting. When all the clouds are sewn down, you may want to add a few machine-embroidered raindrops (as on the back of the vest pictured). Next, use tailor's chalk to draw additional quilting lines across each section. The lines should echo the shapes of the clouds. Using the variously colored threads, sew along the quilting lines with a narrow zigzag stitch.

Using a long straight machine stitch, baste all around the edges of each outer vest section close to the seam line, within the seam allowance. Trim off the excess batting. Assemble and finish the vest and lining, following the pattern directions.

The Pocket

To make a patch pocket like the one pictured on the black satin skirt, cut one large cloud from satin. (Or cut two clouds, overlap them, and sew them together with a zigzag stitch along the overlapping edge; trim away any excess on the wrong side.) Cut a cloud of prequilted fabric the same size for the filling and lining of the pocket. Place the satin and the prequilted clouds together, right sides facing. Using a straight stitch, sew them together all around; make ¼-inch seams and leave a small opening for turning. Turn the cloud right side out. Fold the raw edges of the opening ¼ inch to the inside and press. Stitch this opening closed as near the edge as possible. This may be done by machine, since this stitching will be concealed with the satin stitch. Cut a small cloud appliqué from a contrasting color, coating the edges with diluted glue as for the vest appliqués. Appliqué the small cloud to the pocket, using a satin stitch of the same width as for the vest.

To finish, sew a decorative satin stitch along the edge of the top half of the pocket. Pin the pocket in place on the garment. Beginning and ending where the decorative satin stitching left off, sew the bottom edge of the pocket to the garment using the same satin stitch.

Needlecrafts
Rainbow-cloud quilt $ ▨ ⚹ ♉

The rainbow-cloud quilt, pictured on page 1708, is easily adapted to many sizes and goes together quickly. It is almost entirely stitched by machine, using a variation of the block-by-block quilting method described on page 1703. The clouds, cut from rainbow-striped patchwork fabric, are backed with cloud-shaped pieces of plain fabric to form little pillows, then are sewn onto individual fabric blocks in such a way that the clouds puff up. The quilt shown measures approximately 76 inches square when finished and fits a double bed. To alter the size, add or subtract blocks (each measures 11 inches square when finished), and vary the width of the border strips. (For how to measure a bed for a quilt, see right.) Adjust the fabric requirements and the directions accordingly.

Materials

To make the 76-inch-square quilt, you will need the following amounts of 45-inch-wide cotton, satin, or taffeta fabric: about ½ yard each of eight different colors (for the squares); about ½ yard each of six different colors (for the clouds); 2¾ yards of a dark color for the borders; 6¾ yards of muslin or other inexpensive lightweight fabric (for backing the squares, borders, and clouds); and 4 yards of a color that complements the borders (for the lining). In addition, you will need: a double-bed-sized roll of batting; sewing thread; embroidery thread; sewing needle; sewing machine; large-eyed embroidery needle; cardboard for the patterns; pencil; ruler; bulldog clip; straight pins.

The Clouds

The first step is to make the pillowlike clouds. To begin, make the striped patchwork fabric from which the clouds will be cut. To do this, cut the six fabrics into strips measuring 45 inches long and about 2 inches wide. Sew the strips together with ¼-inch seams, right sides facing, forming a 45-inch-wide piece of striped fabric. For contrast, alternate light-colored stripes with dark ones. Press the seams to one side, preferably toward the darker fabric so the seam allowance does not show through. Enlarge the cloud pattern (Figure R, page 1709) and cut it out of cardboard. Using the pattern, cut out 13 striped clouds (the pattern includes a ¼-inch seam allowance). To save time you can cut several clouds simultaneously. First cut the fabric into thirteen 11-by-12-inch rectangles. Place several rectangles

Q   1 square = ½ inch

Figure Q: Enlarge these cloud patterns by copying them, one square at a time, on paper that you have ruled into ½-inch squares.

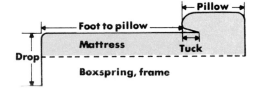

Measuring a bed for a quilt

To measure any bed for a quilt, first measure the width and length of the top of the mattress. The standard twin-bed size is 39 by 75 inches; three-quarter-bed size is 48 by 75 inches; double-bed size is 54 by 75 inches.

To the width and the length of the mattress must be added the drop—that part of the quilt that will hang over the sides and the foot of the bed. The drop may cover just the mattress and box spring, or it may extend to the floor. To make a decorative bedspread-type quilt that will be tucked under the pillow, add 8 inches to the length.

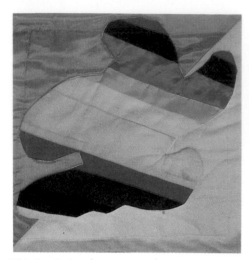

This detail of the rainbow-cloud quilt, pictured at right, shows how the pillowlike clouds puff up.

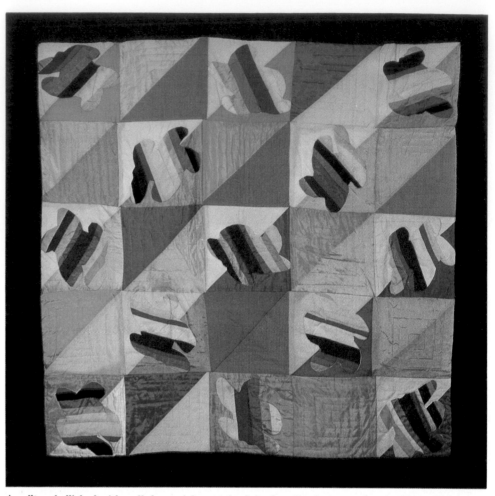

A quilt embellished with puffed-up rainbow-striped cloud appliqués was made using Karen Katz's special techniques. Block-by-block quilting makes the project relatively easy; machine stitching makes the work go fast.

in a pile with the pattern on top; hold them all together at one edge with a bulldog clip. Then cut through the several fabric layers, following the pattern edge. Handle the fabric clouds carefully after you have cut through the seams, since the thread will be unknotted.

Next, cut 13 clouds from muslin, and use one to back each striped cloud by sewing the two together, right sides facing. Make ¼-inch seams and leave a small opening for turning. Turn the cloud right side out and hand sew the opening closed with tiny stitches. You now have 13 little cloud pillows; set them aside until later.

The Squares
Cut a 12-inch square pattern from cardboard. Cut out 25 squares of fabric—about three of each color. Cut each fabric square in half diagonally, forming triangles. Spread the triangles on the floor and mix pieces of different colors to make two-colored squares. As you combine the triangles into five rows of five squares, try to form a dark-light pattern, such as the pattern of diagonal stripes evident in the photograph above. Sew the triangles back together in pairs, forming 25 squares. To do this, place the triangles together, right sides facing, and make a ¼-inch seam. Press the seam to one side, toward the darker-colored triangle.

Quilting
Arrange five rows of five squares. Every other square will have a cloud sewn onto it (see photograph above). Using pencil and ruler, mark quilting lines on the 12 squares that will remain cloudless as follows: Mark a 2-inch square at the center; then make three more concentric squares spaced about 1 inch apart. To mark the

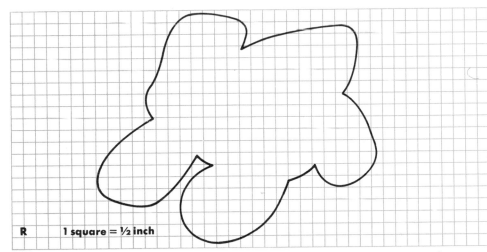

Figure R: To enlarge the cloud pattern for the rainbow-cloud quilt, copy it—one square at a time—on paper that you have ruled in ½-inch squares.

R   1 square = ½ inch

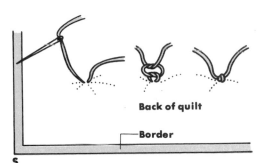

Back of quilt

—Border

S

Figure S: To make a tuft in a quilt, have the lining side of the quilt face up and insert the needle from front to back, penetrating all layers. Taking a tiny stitch, reinsert the needle, and come up about ⅛ inch away from the point of entry. Tie the ends on the back of the quilt, using the square knot shown (right over left, then left over right). Trim the ends to 1 inch.

remaining 13 squares (those that will have clouds sewn on them) draw quilting lines that correspond only to the two outer quilting lines of the cloudless squares (about 2 inches and 3 inches in from the edges). Using the two-colored squares as patterns, cut 25 squares each from the batting and the muslin. Pin the three layers of each square together, and following the directions in the Craftnotes on page 1701, quilt by machine along the marked lines.

When the quilting is done, sew a cloud pillow to each of the 13 lightly quilted blocks. Center each cloud on a block and pin it, face up, to the right side. Machine-stitch all around the cloud's edge, catching just the muslin lining, not the striped top, in the stitching. This is a bit difficult—you will have to keep pushing the top layer away from the needle—but the effect will be worth the trouble, with the clouds puffing up away from the background.

Assembling the Squares and Border

Arrange the blocks once more in five rows of five. You will first assemble five horizontal rows of five blocks each. To sew two blocks together, place them together, right sides facing, and sew with a ¼-inch seam through all six layers. After the five rows have been assembled, press the seam allowances to one side; then sew the rows together, placing them together right sides facing, and again making ¼-inch seams through all six layers. Press the seams to one side.

Next, add the borders. Cut two 12-inch-wide strips of fabric the same length as the sides of the quilt plus 1 inch (this will be approximately 56 inches, but will vary slightly because of the shrinkage caused when you quilted the fabric). Then for the top and bottom borders, cut two 12-inch-wide strips the same length as the patchwork top and bottom, plus 24 inches. Cut batting and backing pieces from muslin the same size as the strips, and baste all six layers together, as for the squares. Machine-quilt three parallel lines along the length of each border strip, spacing the lines 3 inches apart. Right sides facing, sew the side strips to the patchwork, with a ¼-inch seam. Press the seam allowances toward the borders. Then sew the top and bottom border strips to the patchwork and the ends of the side strips. Press the seam allowances toward the borders, and trim any excess fabric at the ends.

Piece the lining fabric together to form a single piece of fabric measuring 3 inches smaller in length and width than the quilt. Baste the lining to the wrong side of the quilt, leaving a 1½-inch margin of excess fabric all around. To hold the quilt and the lining together, the quilt is tufted, or tied, at each corner of the squares. To make a tuft, thread an embroidery needle with two strands of embroidery thread; make a tiny stitch and tie the ends (Figure S). Begin tufting at the center of the quilt and work out toward the edges.

To finish the edges, turn the edges of the front under ¼ inch, and then fold them to the back 1¼ inches. Hand-sew the folded edge to the lining with tiny stitches.

For related entries, see "Appliqué," "Patchwork," and "Machine Stitchery."

RAFFIA AND STRAW
Nature's Bounty

Ruth Straight Hibbs began working with straw as a craft medium when she was young and walked home from school through harvested grain fields in Missouri. She now owns the farmland adjacent to her childhood home. Author of Straw Sculpture, *Ms. Hibbs is also a painter, teacher, and illustrator. She has taught art at Northeast Missouri State University, the University of Colorado, and Cornell University. Her paintings have been widely exhibited.*

For those close to nature at harvest time, straw holds a special fascination. Grains such as wheat, rye, barley, and oats not only provide food but give, in their stems, a medium for craft work. Farmers around the world have traditionally celebrated the bounties of harvest by making straw ornaments—some to present to the gods in gratitude for a plentiful crop, some to give to family and friends, and some to decorate the home at a time of festivity.

Today, of course, straw crafting is not limited to harvest time but can be done the year around. Straw can be woven into serving baskets, tied into amusing animal shapes, crocheted or braided into hats, or cut into pieces for mosaics. The straw you use will be determined by what you are making, and to some extent, where you live—in farming areas the material is often there for the harvesting.

Of the grain straws, wheat and rye straw make the best craft medium because the hollow sections between the nodes—joints in the stem—are quite long. These may be 25 inches long at the top and middle of the plant, though they are much shorter at the base. Each stalk has a head of grain (the plant's seeds) and three or more nodes. A thin husk, attached at each node, is wrapped around the stem for a short bit, then becomes a long thin leaf; husks as well as straw can be used to make split-straw designs. Sections of hollow straw between the nodes are thin near the top of the plant and become thicker toward the bottom, reaching a maximum diameter of ¼ inch. Straws are predominantly golden, though subtle color variations do occur.

Pine straw comes from the longleaf pine also known as the southern pine or the Georgia pine. It produces bundles of needles (the tree's leaves) 12 to 17 inches long. When the leaves are dry, they become pine straw. The longleaf pine grows on the coastal plain from Virginia to Mississippi in a belt about 125 miles wide.

Raffia comes from the leaves of the raffia palm which grows in the forests of Madagascar, off the east coast of Africa. The tree's young leaves are harvested before they turn green, and the transparent outer skin that covers them is stripped off and dried to make long, tough strands of raffia.

Gathering the Straw

If you are harvesting your own straw, do so in early summer when it ripens and turns golden in color (and before rain has discolored it). To harvest the straw of grains, cut the plants near the ground, being careful not to bend the stalks. Spread them in the sun or in an attic to dry. When the straw is dry, cut off the grain heads, and snip out the nodes. Slip off the husks. Sort into bundles of thin, medium, and thick straws, and stand each bundle in a wide-mouthed jar for storage. Before working with the straw, soak it in a pan of water overnight. Prolonged soaking discolors straw, so soak only as much as you plan to use.

Early fall is the best time to gather pine straw, since the trees are shedding then. Arrange the bundles of pine needles with gray sheaths at one end; slip a rubber band around to hold them until needed. Before using, dip the needles into warm water to soften any that may have become brittle. If you do not live where you can do your own harvesting, see the list of suppliers on page 1722.

Grain heads of wheat (top, opposite), a wrinkled strand of raffia (middle), and a cluster of dry pine straw (bottom), lying across a bed of golden wheat straws, are all craft materials provided by nature.

Nineteenth-century drawings of straw plaiting for bonnet making at Luton, England, show cutting the straw (top), sorting the straw (center), and plaiting the straw (bottom).

Split-straw mosaics

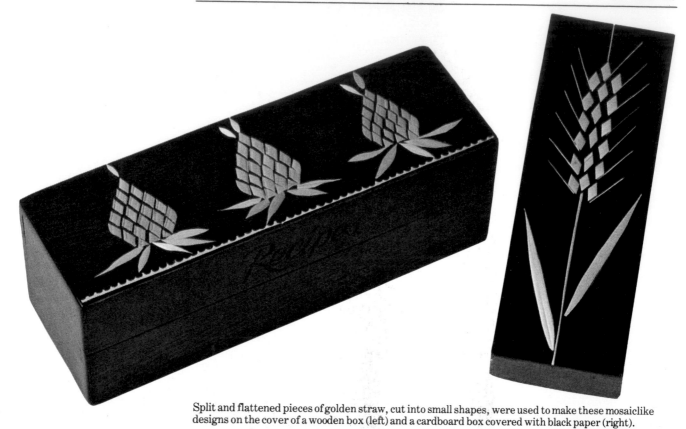

Split and flattened pieces of golden straw, cut into small shapes, were used to make these mosaiclike designs on the cover of a wooden box (left) and a cardboard box covered with black paper (right).

1: Grain heads (left) are removed from un-husked wheat (center). After husking, the tubular pieces of straw remain (right).

2: After soaking the straws overnight, split each straw lengthwise with a craft knife, and press flat with a warm steam iron.

3: Cover one side of each straw—the side that will be the back in the design—with masking tape to prevent splitting when horizontal cuts are made.

4: Use a craft knife to cut small pieces of straw. For more elaborate shapes such as the leaves in the pineapple design, small scissors work well.

Since straws are hollow, they can be split lengthwise and flattened after grain heads and husks have been removed (photograph 1). Mosaic like designs can be made by cutting the flattened strips of straw into small pieces and gluing them onto a surface. The inside of the straw is a lighter color than the outside, but both sides are striated. For variety, the small mosaic pieces can be used with either side up and with the striations running in any direction.

To make split-straw mosaics, select several thick straws, and starting with hot water, soak them overnight. Dry straws are brittle and will crack if they are not soaked first. Split each straw open lengthwise with a craft knife or a razor blade; then press each flat with a warm iron (photograph 2). When the straw is dry, cover the side that will be the back using masking tape (photograph 3) so the straw will not crack when it is cut into small mosaic pieces. Use small, sharp scissors or a craft knife to cut special shapes—triangles, rhomboids, even leaf shapes (photograph 4). Arrange the pieces on a wooden or cardboard box, a piece of fabric, or any flat surface, following the designs pictured opposite or creating your own. When you are pleased with the arrangement, glue the pieces in place with white glue, and let dry overnight.

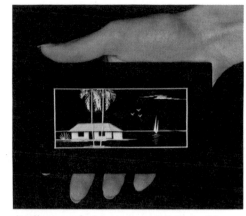

A split-straw design can be as delicate as this miniature tropical scene, made by gluing the straw pieces on a rectangle of black cloth mounted on cardboard.

Weaving, Braiding, and Knotting
Straw giraffes

A menagerie of three-dimensional animals can be created with bent and tied bundles of straw. To make a giraffe (two are pictured below, right), you will need: 25 or 30 thin straws; rubber bands; straw-colored string or No. 10 crochet cotton; and white glue. Select 20 straws, each about 15 inches long. Begin by tying the straws together ½ inch from one end of the bundle, holding them with a rubber band temporarily while you tie. Wrap string around the bundle twice and knot it. To make the head, bend the straws one at a time, beginning ½ inch from the first tie at the throat line. Make subsequent bends gradually farther and farther from the tie so they are about 1 inch from it when you reach the top of the head. Hold the straws and tie them firmly at the neck (photograph 5). If necessary, rearrange the straws to shape the head.

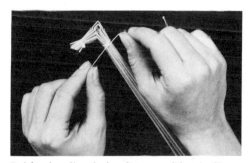

5: After bending the head straws of the giraffe one by one to give a three-dimensional shape to the head, tie the bundle at the neck.

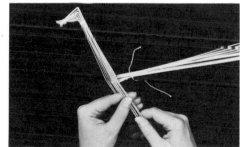

6: Bend the middle straws to make the body, leaving four straws on either side straight to be the front legs. Tie body straws 1 inch from the bend.

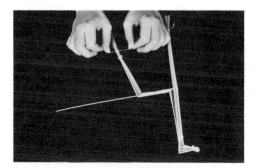

7: Leaving three straws projecting for the tail, bend the body straws to form a pair of back legs. Tie each of the four legs at the ankle.

8: Add extra straws to enlarge the body and back legs; tie them in place. Clip off legs evenly ½ inch below the ankle ties, and braid the tail straws.

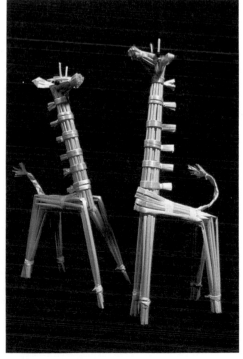

With straws strategically bent and tied together, you can create amusing zoo animals such as these two giraffes with long, slender necks.

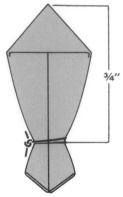

A

Figure A: To make a giraffe ear, fold a wet and flattened straw twice to make a point, and tie ¾ inch from this tip. Clip off excess straw at an angle below the tie, and glue the ear into the head straws.

To make the back, make another series of sharp bends in the opposite direction 4 inches below the tie at the top of the neck. Leave four straight straws on each side of the body to be the front legs (photograph 6). Tie the bent straws 1 inch behind the legs. For the back legs, bend the body straws downward 2 inches beyond the body tie, leaving three straws projecting in the middle for the tail. Tie the front and back legs at the ankle line 2½ inches down from the body (photograph 7). To give the body and back legs added thickness, fold four extra straws in half, and wrap them around the front of the body; then bend them at the hip to join the back legs. (If a thin floral wire is run through the hollow center of one of these straws before it is bent, it will help hold the back legs in position.) Tie the four added straws to the ankle; clip the straws evenly ½ inch below the ankle ties. Braid the projecting straws to make the tail (photograph 8). With the exception of the eyes, which are black-headed map pins, features are all made with short pieces of straw. For horns, push ¾-inch pieces of straw, dipped into glue, between the head straws. To make the ears, flatten two pieces of wet straw, fold them to points, tie them ¾ inch from the tip, and cut off excess straw (Figure A). Put glue on the squared-off ends, and push them into the sides of the head. For the neck mane, fold six 3-inch wet and flattened straws in half. Fit them around the neck at evenly spaced intervals, and tie them in place. For a more natural look, you can cover the string with raffia. Trim the straws to a uniform length. Other animals can be made with the same techniques by modifying the identifying characteristics.

Weaving, Braiding, and Knotting
Straw hat

The hat of hand-braided straw has a flat-topped crown, a brim wider in the front than in the back, and a flowerlike decoration made of braided palmetto strips.

At harvest time, pioneer women made straw hats for their families, taking sheaves of wheat straw into the house to be husked and soaked. The children helped by flattening the straws which were then braided, coiled, and stitched to fit each individual. To make a straw hat like the one pictured at left, you will need ¼ pound of straw; string or No. 10 crochet cotton; straight and curved darning needles; enough grosgrain ribbon to circle your head; and materials for trimming. Choose long, thick straws of uniform thickness but uneven length. Soak the straws overnight; then flatten them with a heavy weight such as a brick. To start a braid, use wet straws and lay out a horizontal row of five straws topped by a vertical row of four straws (Figure B). Tape these together to hold them in position as you braid, following Figure B. You will make a continuous braid 1¼ inches wide and about 230 inches long. As each straw is used up, lay another flattened straw on top of it, and continue braiding. Overlap the straws at each splice—excess straw can be neatly trimmed off later. To forestall weak spots in the braid, avoid splicing two straws at the same point (the reason for using straws of unequal lengths). If braiding is interrupted long enough so the straw dries, resoak the unfinished part before starting to braid again. When the braid is completed, stitch over both ends so they do not unravel. If the braid dries before you begin turning it into a hat, soak it again for about half an hour.

Begin making the hat at the center of the crown. Use a straight darning needle to insert a double thickness of string or crochet cotton between layers of wet straw on one edge of the braid (Figure C). Thread through 6 inches of braid at first; then pull on the string until the threaded edge of the braid is pulled into a tight curve (Figure C). Keep advancing the thread and pulling. When the first circle is completed, press it with a warm iron until it is fairly dry. Working inside the crown, stitch the edges of braid together as you continue to spiral outward (Figure D). Stitch carefully so the string is not visible from the outside. Press each row to keep the crown flat. After the braid has gone around three times, begin to pull tightly on the drawstring so the crown begins to shape to the head. Try the hat on frequently to make sure you get a comfortable fit. When the crown is finished, knot both the gathering string and the sewing string. Use the darning needle to put another string around the bottom edge of the braid, and pull it in to a comfortable fit; then fasten the string by taking a few stitches. Knot and clip off the excess. Press this crown edge until it is dry.

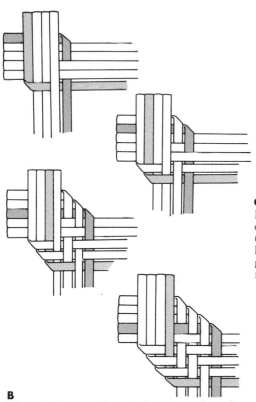

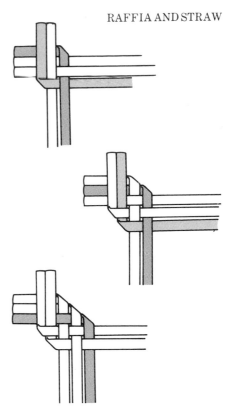

B

Figure B: Arrange nine wet, flat straws of equal thickness but uneven lengths, as diagrammed. Tape or stitch the ends together. Bend the first horizontal straw, and weave it over two straws and under two straws; then do the same with the first vertical straw (top). Continue braiding this way, weaving first the horizontal straw, then the vertical, as shown in the next three drawings. As each straw is used up, introduce a new one by overlapping the old one.

Figure C: To start the crown of the hat, thread a doubled string through one edge of the braid (upper left) for 6 inches or so. Pull tight until you have formed a tight circle (lower right). Then begin stitching the edges together with a curved needle and thread.

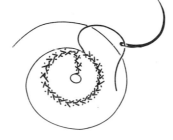

D

Figure D: Working on the inside of the crown, stitch the edge of the braid as you continue to spiral it around, shaping the crown as you go. Use a curved upholstery needle, and make stitches that do not show on the outside of the hat by hiding them in the braid.

E

Figure E: To make braid trim for the brim and crown, arrange five wet, flat straws as shown. Tape or stitch the ends. Bend the first horizontal straw, and weave it over one straw and under the next; then do the same with the first vertical straw (top). Continue braiding in this way, weaving over one straw and under the next (next two drawings). Splice in new straws as needed.

9: Sew a narrow reinforcing braid on the inside edge of the hat brim. Then as a sweatband, sew a 1-inch-wide grosgrain ribbon around the base of the crown.

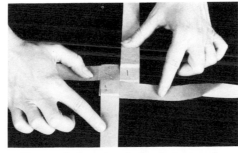

10: To start the hat trim of palmetto leaves, place four strips at right angles to each other, starting with the top strip and working clockwise. Staple them together where they overlap.

11: Fold the strips over the center one by one, working clockwise from the top. Do not crease the ends of the loops you make, since you want a fat, square braid.

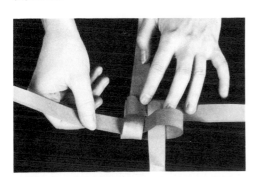

12: Slip the end of the fourth strip through the loop made by the first strip and pull firmly, locking the loop in place.

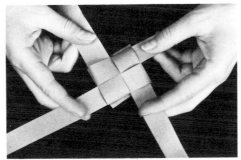

13: Then pull all four ends firmly to lock this layer of the braid. Continue weaving in the same way until the flowerlike braid is finished.

14: Twist pipe-cleaner stems around palmetto braids, wrap the pipe cleaner with masking tape, loop grosgrain ribbon around the stem; sew to hat.

To make the brim without cutting the braid, continue spiraling and catch-stitching from the inside. With the aid of a drawstring, keep the braid flat as the brim progresses; press frequently. Make the brim four braid widths wide in front and three in back. (A straw hat is more interesting if the brim is wider at the front.) To achieve this, spiral the braid gradually inward as you near the edge of the brim. End it under the brim (photograph 9), and stitch across the end of the braid. To reinforce the edge of the brim, make a five-strand braid from thin wet straws (Figure E). Make it long enough to go around the edge of the brim, and also around the base of the crown as a hatband. Stitch a portion of this braid to the bottom of the outer edge of the brim, being careful not to let the stitches show on the outside. Fit the remaining portion of this braid around the crown, and sew the ends together. For a sweatband, stitch a length of grosgrain ribbon inside the crown where it meets the brim (photograph 9).

The trim on the hat pictured is made from palmetto strips plaited into square braids. For this you will need: 12 palmetto strips; three pipe cleaners; masking tape; and 8 inches of grosgrain ribbon. To make the trim, overlap the wide ends of four palmetto strips at right angles, and staple them together (photograph 10). Fold the strips back over the center one by one, going clockwise (photograph 11). Slip the end of the fourth strip into the loop made by the first strip (photograph 12), thus locking the fourth strand in place. Pull the ends firmly (photograph 13). Continue plaiting until the strips are almost used up. The braid will become smaller as the palmetto strips become narrower. Twist a pipe cleaner onto the base ends of the braid, and wrap it neatly with narrow masking tape—to simulate a stem. Make three of these palmetto braids, stitch a length of grosgrain ribbon around them, as shown, and attach them to the side of the hat. Cut the ends of the ribbon into an inverted V shape (photograph 14). Alternatively, you could use artificial flowers as a trim or simply tie a bow with grosgrain ribbon.

Needlecrafts
Crocheted raffia belt

15: Natural raffia comes in straw-colored strands that are strong but very supple, even when dry.

Circles to encircle your waist are crocheted into a belt using strands of raffia, a fiber from palm-tree leafstalks. The belt is fastened with a cord inserted through the centers of the end circles.

The suppleness and strength of natural raffia (photograph 15) make it excellent for crocheted work such as the belt pictured above. The long, straw-colored strands are easy to crochet, and they are supple enough to use dry. To make the belt, crochet a chain (see Craftnotes opposite) equal to your waist measurement plus 3 inches. (The extra inches allow for the take-up that occurs when the circular motifs are added.) At the end of the chain, turn back and work 6 dc (see Craftnotes for abbreviations) into the 3rd chain from the hook. *Skip 2 ch, sl st in next ch; skip 2 ch, work 6 dc into next ch . Repeat from * until the chain is used up. Turn, and repeat this pattern on the other side of the original row of chain stitches, thus making a series of attached circles.

Fasten the belt at the center front with a cord or ribbon inserted into the center holes of the end circles.

CRAFTNOTES: CROCHET STITCHES

Chain stitch

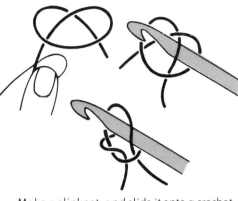

Make a slipknot, and slide it onto a crochet hook.

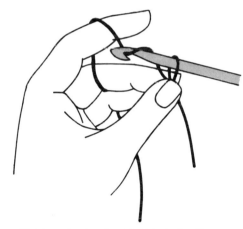

Hold crochet hook with right index finger and thumb (left if you're left-handed). Wrap yarn through fingers of other hand to provide tension, and guide with index finger. Bring yarn over and around crochet hook.

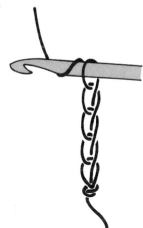

Catch yarn on hook (called yarn over) and pull through existing loop. Original loop slips off. Repeat for foundation chain.

Slip stitch

Insert hook in top strand of the stitch below.

Yarn over, and draw through both loops on hook.

Single crochet

Insert hook into the stitch below.

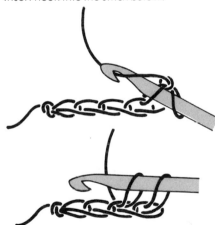

Yarn over (top), and draw through stitch so there are 2 loops on hook (bottom).

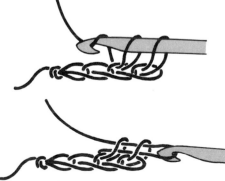

Yarn over (top), and draw yarn through both loops (bottom).

Double crochet

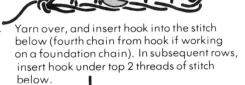

Yarn over, and insert hook into the stitch below (fourth chain from hook if working on a foundation chain). In subsequent rows, insert hook under top 2 threads of stitch below.

Draw up loop so there are 3 loops on hook.

Yarn over, and pull through 2 loops.

Two loops remain on hook.

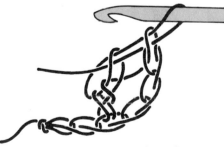

Yarn over, and pull through last 2 loops.

Abbreviations

ch	chain
dc	double crochet
*	repeat from
rnd	round
sc	single crochet
sl st	slip stitch
st(s)	stitch(es)
yo	yarn over

Crocheted raffia makes a sporty combination when it is used in a visor cap and a fringed shoulder bag. The bag is really made of brown denim, concealed by raffia decorations.

Needlecrafts
Raffia shoulder bag

Although the shoulder bag (left) looks as though it is made entirely of raffia, it is actually a brown denim bag on which crocheted raffia decorations have been sewn. To make the bag, you will need: ¼ pound of raffia; a size E crochet hook; two 3-inch round perforated plastic forms (see Suppliers, page 1722); five rectangular perforated plastic forms, ¾ by 9 inches; ½ yard of denim; large-eyed needle; and thread.

To make the denim bag, cut four circles 9 inches in diameter and two strips 3 by 54 inches (seam where necessary). With right sides facing, stitch two circles together ½ inch from the edge, leaving a 2-inch opening. Trim the seam, turn right side out, and stitch the opening closed by hand. Repeat with the other two circles.

16: To start the round decoration for the shoulder bag, cover a round plastic form with raffia, using cross stitches around the edge (above), then radiating straight stitches into the center.

17: Cover the narrow plastic forms with raffia, using a slanted stitch. To attach the fringe, put raffia loops through the plastic; then pull the raffia ends through the loops. Attach to denim as shown.

Stitch the two strips together, right sides facing, to form a long tube. Trim the seam, turn right side out, and press. Stitch the raw ends together to form a loop. This will be the handle as well as the gusset between the circles. With the last seam in the tube at the bottom of the bag, stitch the tube and the two circles together (Figure F). Leave an 8-inch-long arc open at the top of the bag.

To start the circular raffia decorations, cover the round plastic form with raffia, using cross stitches around the edge (photograph 16) and radiating straight stitches in the center. When the plastic is covered, start the crochet (see Craftnotes, page 1717). Row 1: Work 1 sc into each hole in the plastic form. Row 2: Dc into each sc. Row 3: Sc into each dc. Row 4: Sc into each sc. Row 5: Ch 4, skip 2 sc, *dc, ch 2, skip 2 sc. Repeat from * around the circle. Row 6: Sc into each dc and each ch. Row 7: Dc into each sc. Row 8: Sc into each dc. Fasten off. This makes a circle approximately 8½ inches in diameter. Make a second circle for the other side of the bag. Stitch both circles onto the denim bag.

To make the shoulder-strap ornamentation, cover and join the narrow, plastic forms with raffia. Then stitch them to the denim strap (photograph 17). To make the fringe, fold a 4-inch strand of raffia in half, push the loop through a hole at the end of the plastic form, put the raffia ends through this loop, and pull tight. Each of the six fringes on the bottom of the bag is made by threading 8-inch-long strands of raffia into a large-eyed needle and stitching them into the denim. Put the needle in from the outside of the bag, and come out again about 1 inch away. Repeat six times at intervals along the bottom of the bag; then tie together the free ends of the strands of raffia in each fringe about 1 inch below the bag.

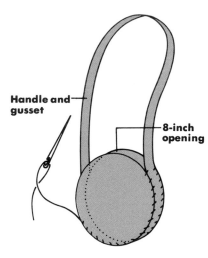

Handle and gusset

8-inch opening

F

Figure F: To assemble the denim shoulder bag, stitch the two 8-inch circles to the long gusset-and-handle loop, leaving an opening at the top of the bag.

Needlecrafts
Crocheted visor cap

A raffia cap is just the thing to keep the bright summer sun out of your eyes. The cap is simple to make and can be adjusted to fit your head exactly. You will need ¼ pound of raffia, a size E crochet hook, and two ½-inch plastic curtain rings.

Crocheting the Cap

Chain 3 and join together with a sl st (see Craftnotes, page 1717). Work 6 dc into the ring. Continue working dc around in a circle (photograph 18), fitting the cap to your head as you crochet. When the cap is the right size, work a row of dc halfway around the cap—to begin the visor—occasionally taking two stitches in one place so the visor fans out slightly. Without cutting the raffia strand, double back on the visor and work 1 sl st, 1 sc. Then work a row of dc to within the last two stitches of the visor. Work 1 sc, 1 sl st to taper the visor front. Continue the sc around the back of the cap and up the other side of the visor. Then when you reach the dc on the visor, change to dc and work the third row of the visor. At the side of the visor, again change to sc to taper the side, and end with a sl st. Repeat these rows just along the visor without working around the entire cap. Work five or six rows depending on how deep you want the visor. As you crochet, try on the cap; then shape and press with a warm iron.

To decorate the cap, make a three-strand braid of raffia. Cover the two curtain rings with raffia strips that have been split lengthwise. Double a thin strip in its center, and slip the loop through the ring. Pull the free ends of the raffia strip through the loop, securing the raffia strip to the ring. Continue looping the raffia through the ring and pulling the end through the loop, as in a buttonhole stitch, until the ring is completely covered. Take a small stitch in the last loop, and knot these ends on the underside. Make a three-strand raffia braid long enough to fit around the crown from one side of the visor to the other. Attach a raffia-covered curtain ring to each end of the braid by overlapping the braid and stitching it. Then stitch the decoration to the cap.

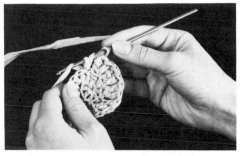

18: To make the crown of the visor cap, work double crochet stitches into a ring; spiral round and round until the crown is large enough to fit your head.

Needlecrafts
Woven raffia earrings

You can make earrings quickly by covering a curtain ring with raffia and weaving thin strands of raffia in the center. You will need: raffia; two 1¼-inch non-metallic curtain rings (metal causes raffia to turn green); and screw-on or pierced earring wires, available at craft stores and jewelry supply houses.

To cover a curtain ring, double a strand of raffia, and put the resulting loop through the ring. Push the free ends of raffia through the loop and pull tight (photograph 19). Continue looping the raffia around the ring until the ring is covered. Then, using a thin but tough strand of raffia, thread a large-eyed needle, and make a series of spokes across the center of the circle (photograph 20). Begin each stitch at the edge, cross the center of the circle, and end at the opposite edge. The result will be an even number of spokes. Since an odd number of spokes is needed for weaving, bring the last strand just to the center, and start weaving it under and over the spokes (photograph 21) until the center has been circled four times. Take a final stitch into the woven area, and secure it with a knot on the underside.

Attach the completed raffia-covered ring to the earring wire with a small piece of raffia. Repeat for the other earring.

Raffia-covered curtain rings make unique earrings to wear in the summer.

19: To begin a raffia earring, double a strand of raffia and pull the loop through a curtain ring. Put the free ends of raffia through the loop and pull tight.

20: To make the spokes of the earring, stitch thin raffia from edge to edge across the center of the raffia-covered ring, making ten spokes that cross in the center.

21: After making the spokes, bring the raffia to the center of the ring to form the eleventh spoke; then weave the raffia over and under the spokes until you have circled the center four times.

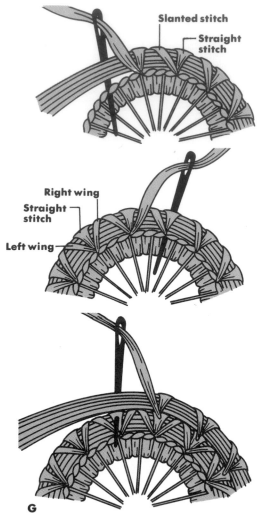

G

Figure G: To start a wing stitch, take the raffia through the edge of the ring, around the pine straw, and back through the same hole, forming a straight stitch (top). Wrap the raffia around the straw again, but take the second stitch to the left, forming a slanted stitch (top). Continue alternating straight and slanted stitches until you have circled the center once. Then reverse the direction, putting the needle back through the same holes around the ring but making only slanted stitches, the right wings (center). In the second and subsequent rows, stitch into the center of the straight stitch below, splitting the raffia (bottom).

H

Figure H: Place the raffia-covered wire around the paper pattern, matching the circumference of the tray, and mark off the eight equal arcs on the wire.

1720

Weaving, Braiding, and Knotting
Round tray

Craftspeople of the southeastern United States, where the longleaf pine is abundant, make baskets and trays of pine straw (photograph 22) held together with raffia. The trays pictured opposite were made with this technique. To make the round tray, you will need two ounces of pine straw, one ounce of raffia, a thin tapestry needle, one 1¼-inch non-metallic curtain ring, and 30 inches of 18-gauge wire.

Making the Base

To start the base, cover the curtain ring with raffia, following the instructions given for the earrings on page 1719. Then group four clusters of pine needles, with the sharp ends pointing the same way, and slip off the gray end-sheaths. Split a piece of raffia in half lengthwise. Thread half into a large-eyed needle and begin spiraling the bundles of pine straw around the center ring, stitching them in place with a wing stitch. (If you are right-handed, coil the pine straw in a counterclockwise direction so that the left hand can guide them while the right hand sews; if you are left-handed, coil the pine straw in a clockwise direction.) To begin a wing stitch, take a stitch from the back into the raffia on the edge of the center ring (photograph 23). Wrap the strand of raffia around the bundle of pine straw, and stitch it back into the first needle hole. This secures the bundle with a straight stitch (Figure G, top). Wrap the raffia around the straw cluster again, but take the stitch a short distance to the left of the first; this makes a slanted stitch. Again, wrap the raffia around the bundle of pine straw and insert the needle into the second needle hole with another straight stitch. Continue this pattern of straight and slanted stitches (photograph 24) until you have circled the ring. Then, in order to make the other wing on each stitch, reverse your direction, and go back once through each needle hole, making single slanted stitches that are right wings (Figure G, center). When you get back to the starting point, make the second round as you did the first. On all rounds after the first, stitch into the center of the straight stitch below, splitting the raffia (Figure G, bottom). This splitting of the straight stitches is decorative,

22: Pine straw comes from the needles of the longleaf pine. A branch is shown at the top and left, separated needle clusters at the right.

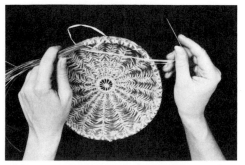

23: To begin making a tray with wing stitches, take a stitch into the edge of the raffia-covered ring from the back of the ring.

24: Use raffia in the wing stitch design to hold bundles of pine straw to the edge of the raffia-covered curtain ring.

25: Develop the sides of the tray by adding bundles of pine straw at right angles to the flat base circle.

keeps the rows of straight stitches aligned, and keeps slanted stitches from slipping between layers of pine needles. When you near the end of the first bundle of pine straw, intermingle the pointed tips with the base ends of another bundle of four clusters of pine needles, and continue stitching. When the base is approximately 6¾ inches across, begin to develop raised sides by attaching the bundles of pine straw atop the edge of the base. Continue building layers of pine straw until the sides are 1 inch high (photograph 25). Then gradually taper the bundle of pine straw to an even finish.

The Scalloped Border

To make the trim, put the tray top down on a piece of paper, and trace around it to get the circumference. Divide the resulting circle evenly into eighths as a guide in making scallops. For the scallops, cut a 30-inch length of 18-gauge wire, and shape it into a circle, twisting the ends together. Wrap the wire with several layers of raffia, and secure it with masking tape. Place the wire around the circle you drew on paper, and mark off the eighths on the wire (Figure H). Then shape each eighth into a scallop deep enough so it will touch the rim of the tray (photograph 26). Stitch four rounds of pine straw to the raffia-covered wire scallops, using the wing stitch that

26: After marking the raffia-covered wire into eight equal parts, shape each section into a scallop. Make indentations deep enough so all will touch the rim of the basket.

27: Stitch four rows of pine straw clusters onto the outer edge of the raffia-covered wire scallops, using the same wing stitch that was used for the tray itself.

These shallow trays are made of clusters of pine straw, held together with decorative raffia stitches. The centers are raffia-covered curtain rings. The round tray is decorated with fanlike scallops. The oval tray has Australian pine cones inserted into the handles.

Suppliers of straw and raffia

Wheat straw:
Maid of Scandinavia Company
3244 Raleigh Avenue
Minneapolis, Minnesota 55416

Paul Straight Craft Supplies
Yarrow, Missouri 63501

Pine straw:
Ruth Straight Hibbs
115 Chelsea Circle
Statesboro, Georgia 30458

Raffia:
American Handicraft Company
1011 Foch Street
Fort Worth, Texas 76107

Cane and Basket Supply Company
1283 South Cochran Avenue
Los Angeles, California 90019

Craftsman Supply House
35 Brown's Avenue
Scottsville, New York 14546

Plastic open-grill forms:
Bazaar Novelty Co.
Miami, Florida 33138

Craftsman Supply House
Maid of Scandinavia Company

was used for the body of the tray (photograph 27). To attach the finished border to the tray, stitch the eight innermost points of the scallops to the rim of the tray using raffia. The border will have eight semicircular openings, the inside of the scallops, which can be left open or filled in with raffia.

Filling the Scallops

A decorative way to finish the scalloped border is to fill in the semicircular openings with fans of raffia (Figure I). To make a fan, push a needle threaded with raffia through the edge of the basket from the outside at the center of a semicircular opening, with the knot on the outside. Carry the strip of raffia to the right inside edge of the scallop. Put the needle in from the top and come out again a short distance to the left. Bring the needle back to the basket edge in the center of the scallop. Continue stitching spokes, moving to the left, until the scallop is filled with an odd number of spokes. End with the needle at the original hole in the basket edge. Without cutting the raffia, weave under and over all the spokes twice (Figure I, right). Push the needle down through the original hole, and knot at the back. When all the fans have been made, the tray is finished.

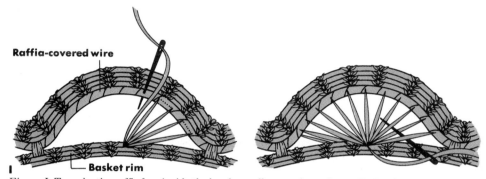

Raffia-covered wire

Basket rim

Figure I: To make the raffia fans inside the border scallops, make spokes radiating from the center of the semicircle (left). After completing the last spoke, bring the raffia to the center hole again; then weave the raffia over and under the spokes once (right).

Weaving, Braiding, and Knotting
Oval tray
$ ⊠ ⚔ 🧺

The oval tray pictured at left on page 1721 is made the same way as the round tray. The shape is different because the tray was started with three covered rings instead of one. You will need: two ounces of pine straw; one ounce of raffia; three 1¼-inch non-metallic curtain rings; and a tapestry needle. The small pine-cone decorations are optional; you could use a raffia fan stitch instead, similar to the one used on the round tray.

Cover and decorate the three curtain rings with raffia, following the directions on page 1719. With raffia, sew the three rings together in a row. Spiral four-cluster bundles of pine straw around the three-ring center, using the wing stitch (Figure G, page 1720), until the oval measures approximately 5¼ by 7½ inches.

Build up the sides to a height of ¾ inch. To make a handle, let a cluster of pine straw swing free from the body of the tray near one end of the oval. Reattach at the matching point on the opposite side, and continue attaching the cluster to the side with wing stitches. (If you plan to insert pine cones in the handle space, measure to make sure they will fit.) When you reach the other end of the oval, make the second handle. Continue spiraling for five or six more rounds to give width to the handles. Taper the final bundle of pine straw to a neat finish.

The spaces between the handles and the body of the tray may be left unadorned, decorated with raffia stitches, or filled in with small round and oval wooden beads. In the tray pictured, several sizes of Australian pine cones are held in place with the thin strands of raffia that encage them. These cones have small end-to-end projections that grip the raffia strands. The method of attaching pine straw with raffia used in these trays can also be used to make many flat items, such as coasters and placemats, by omitting the sides.

Needlecrafts
Pine-straw envelope purse $ ▯ ⚹ ⚙

Pine straw can be woven into needlepoint canvas in much the same way as yarn. The purse pictured below, right, was made this way from a 10½-by-13½-inch piece of ecru-colored 10-mesh penelope canvas, one ounce of pine straw, ½ yard of acetate fabric in a matching color for the lining, and needle and thread.

Use pine straw that has been freshly gathered, if possible. Otherwise dampen the straw before use so it will not break when bent. Also, run your thumbnail along the dull side of each straw to relax the strip before weaving it. Keep the shiny side facing out as you weave. Use the pointed end of each strip to weave it in and out of the canvas—there is no need to use a needle. If the tip blunts or breaks, clip it to a new point using a small scissors.

To make the plain stripes in the purse, weave the straw into the canvas as shown (photograph 28). To make the decorative stripes, weave a series of sunburst rectangles in which the stitches radiate from a central point (photograph 29). Use an awl or nail to enlarge this hole when it becomes too crowded with straw. Turn the needlepoint canvas under ¼ inch on all four sides, and use a whip stitch to finish these edges.

For the lining, cut a piece of fabric 17½ by 20 inches. Fold it in half to make a 10-by-17½-inch rectangle. Using a ¼-inch seam, stitch around this rectangle, leaving a 3-inch opening. Turn the lining right side out, stitch the opening closed, and press. The resulting rectangle, 9½ by 17 inches, has the right side of the fabric exposed on both sides and has all four edges finished. Place the lining on top of the wrong side of the needlepoint purse (Figure J) so top and bottom edges meet and the sides of the lining extend 2 inches beyond the needlepoint canvas on both sides. Stitch the lining to the canvas. The side extensions will form the gussets which make the envelope expandable. Fold these gussets in on top of the lining, and stitch the edges down 8 inches from the top (the length of the 3-inch flap plus the 5-inch envelope back). Bring the edge of the remaining 5 inches of lining up to the 5 inches directly above it, and stitch down—thus forming the 5-inch-deep envelope.

For related entries, see "Braided Rugs," "Basketry," and "Weaving."

28: To make the plain stripes that decorate the needlepoint clutch bag, weave pine straw in an over-and-under pattern.

29: To make sunburst stripes for the bag, make stitches of pine straw that radiate out from the center to the edge of a rectangle.

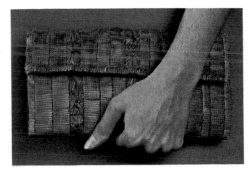

The envelope purse is made of needlepoint canvas stitched with pine straw instead of yarn. It has a fabric lining with a pocket to hold your valuables.

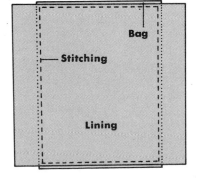

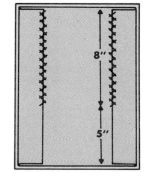

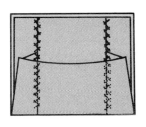

J
Figure J: Place the lining over the wrong side of the needlepoint canvas purse so 2 inches of lining fabric extend on either side of the canvas; then stitch the lining in place (far left). Fold the side extensions in on top of the lining, and stitch down 8 inches from the top (left center). Bring the edge of the bottom 5 inches of lining and canvas up, and stitch it in place to form the pocket (near left).

RAG DOLLS
The Cuddly People

Remember your rag doll? You took it to bed with you every night and cuddled it in your arms. It was your best friend; but after awhile it became kind of funny looking, with one eye missing, some stitches coming loose, and the stuffing beginning to spill out. You tried to mend it but your mother said it was too dirty and you would have to give it up. That was a sad day, the day you put away your favorite rag doll. Maybe it was made from a sock or a stocking or an old piece of muslin. Most likely it was dressed in fabric that had once been someone's favorite dress. Perhaps your grandmother made it especially for you. If so, it was all the more special; a doll that is made by one person for another is a true expression of love.

Rag dolls are different from other kinds of dolls. Unlike the streamlined modern types with their elegant wardrobes and fabulous accessories, rag dolls do not walk, talk, wet, eat, cry, or close their eyes. But somehow, perhaps because they leave so much to the imagination, they seem more like real people than the other kind. Rag dolls made of familiar materials fill almost anyone with nostalgia. Old socks and stockings, junk trimmings from the sewing box, scraps of fabric, old clothes, even the rags that are the traditional stuffing, were all once part of someone's life before they wore out.

I began making dolls when I was a child, and I still have some of those early efforts. Today, I make dolls for both children and adults; they range from the simplest of abstract forms to fully developed caricatures that are sometimes called soft sculpture. Whatever you choose to call them, they are all rag dolls at heart.

Andrea Rubrum is a multimedia artisan skilled in sculpture, painting, drawing, ceramics, and batik. She designs and makes appliqué clothing and theatrical sets, created a puppet film for UNICEF, and helped produce two TV films on young people in the arts. Her work has been exhibited in many New York galleries, including Fairtree Gallery and the Museum of Contemporary Crafts.

Figure A: Starting with an arch shape (above, left), create your own design freehand on paper before you begin to cut, sew, and stuff. Two-dimensional arms and legs can be tacked into the seams.

Pick a Personality

To create a doll, I begin with a mental picture of a specific person or a type of person. A rag doll needs a very definite personality, and though you can alter the design as you go along, it is good to have some idea of the kind of person the doll may become before you start. Will it be old or young, fancy or plain? Will it be a he or a she or a neuter? What kind of features makes it what it is? Is it the big nose, a certain kind of hair style, or big feet? Did you see someone at the movies or riding home on the bus who would make a good-looking doll? ("What a doll!" you may have exclaimed.) Once you have some idea of what you want the doll to be like, take inventory of the materials you have available—buttons, ribbons, lace, feathers, fabric—anything that could become part of the design. Gather it all together, with needle, thread, scissors, pencil, and paper.

Rag dolls need not be lifelike forms. Start by sketching some basic shapes and faces; you will find that it is easy and fun to create and draw your own pattern designs freehand. In Figures A and B above, you can see how a simple shape can progress from outline to personality. Try sketching an arch shape and developing your own face and costume. On the next page you will see a variety of arch-shaped dolls.

Figure B: Starting with an A-shaped variation of the basic arch shape (top, left), draw arms and legs into the pattern to create more lifelike dolls.

Andrea Rubrum enjoys a doll maker's holiday nestled among a few of the many rag dolls she has created. For a closer look at the characters in this rag's gallery, turn the pages.

Needlecrafts
Rag dolls for everyone

These dolls display a range of personalities created with simple variations on the same basic arch shape. From left to right: a feather-top doll with felt strip arms and legs; another featherhead with arms made from stuffed white-cotton gloves; a lady doll whose arms and feet were drawn into the pattern; a reversible doll whose pirate half on the other side appears on page 1724.

Memorable rag doll designs can be inspired by a child's drawing, like the blue denim redhead above.

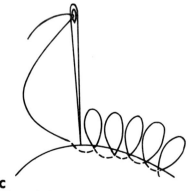

C

Figure C: To create curly hair, make a continuous loop stitch of yarn.

Arch-Shaped Dolls

I love arch-shaped rag dolls because they are little people pillows, soft and simple. Whether or not they have arms and legs, they remain basically all body. Still, there is quite a lot you can do in modifying the shape.

If you are making a doll for a young child, the child's own artwork is one of the best places to look for inspiration. My niece Erica's drawing, above, suggested the shape for the little blue denim doll next to it. The pattern was drawn freehand right on the fabric. Cut two pieces of any shape you draw, for front and back, and stitch almost completely around the shape, right sides facing, leaving a ¼-inch seam allowance. Turn the doll right side out and stuff it with polyester filling, cotton batting, rags, or kapok. As a general rule, I avoid shredded foam-rubber stuffing because it gets lumpy and tends to decompose after a while. Turn the edges of the open seam under, and finish the seam with hand stitches.

You can create faces with embroidery and appliqué, tints of vegetable dye, or felt markers. Make curly hair with yarn looped with a slip stitch (Figure C). Extra touches, like the appliquéd heart on the blue denim doll, seem like little things but they make a doll especially endearing.

The line-up of dolls at the top of the page, opposite, may give you ideas for your own creations. The pink-feather-haired girl in the flowered dress (left) has arms and legs cut from strips of felt stitched into the seams (Figure A, page 1725). Then, since she was made for a teen-ager, I stitched on rows of sequins to make rings and a bracelet and created her face with dime-store eyes (the kind with pupils that roll around), a row of stitches for a mouth, and a tint of rouge. When you make a doll for a child, use only button eyes and beads that can be sewn on securely; anything that can be pulled off and swallowed is dangerous.

A pair of cotton gloves from a thrift shop, stuffed and sewed to the sides of the doll second from left, opposite, gave it wonderful arms and hands. Her sparkly dress was pieced together with bits of fabric and trimmings. But the personality did not really emerge until I gave her that shock of feather hair.

When I drew the pattern with feet and hands shown in Figure B, page 1725, the A shape suggested a dress to me. So I incorporated this idea into the design of the party doll, third from left, opposite. She has an evening gown of cut velvet edged with antique braid, earrings of crocheted lace, and hair of black yarn stitched on in loops (Figure C).

There is more to the doll at right, opposite, than meets the eye. A sweet young thing is on one side, but when you turn the doll over, there is a one-eyed pirate to startle you (see page 1724). The wig, made from a single piece of black mohair, serves them both. The faces were created with a combination of embroidery, appliqué, lines drawn on with felt-tipped markers, and food coloring or dyes.

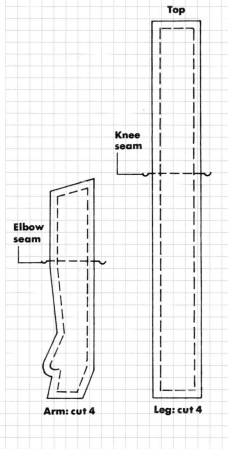

Top

Knee seam

Elbow seam

Arm: cut 4   **Leg: cut 4**

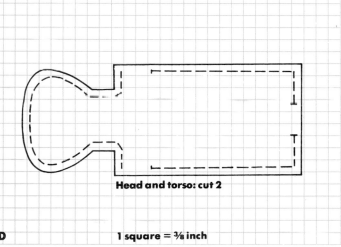

Head and torso: cut 2

D   1 square = ⅜ inch

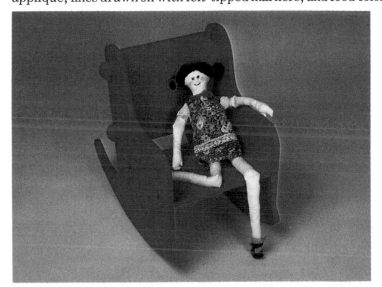

Mary Jane, a gangly jointed rag doll, is stitched across the knees and elbows so it is easy for her to lounge in a red rocker.

Figure D: To enlarge this jointed doll pattern, draw a grid of ⅜-inch squares; then copy the lines in each small square into the corresponding larger square.

Jointed Rag Dolls

Jointed dolls, a bit more complex than the arch-shapes, are more animated. But they are still very simple to design and sew. Long-legged Mary Jane, above, is cut from the pattern in Figure D. The shape is open to all kinds of variations; limbs and torso can be thinner or fatter, longer or shorter; the fabric used can be printed or plain. When all the pieces have been cut, sewn, and stuffed individually, sew the legs and arms onto the torso. Then make the joints by sewing straight across the stuffed fabric at the seam lines indicated for elbows and knees. In this case the doll's dress was made separately. I pieced it together without a pattern, draping, pinning, cutting, basting, and adding trim as I went along.

This long-waisted two-in-one doll has a secret self that will appear when the doll is flipped upside down, reversing the double skirts.

Two-in-One Doll

Children have always loved dolls with more than one face, dolls that can express different emotions or represent different people. The pirate-and-girl combination is one such doll; pictured left is another type, popular in colonial times. With a flip of the long skirt, a second doll is revealed and the first disappears (Figure E). The pattern could be modified so the shape of each side is different, but I made matching halves, like barbells, so the hands give the skirt a hoop-skirt look on either side. Note that the doll has two waistlines and two skirts, necessary to keep the proportions right. I used felt-tipped markers to draw the faces and parts of the costumes right on the fabric. Other ideas for a two-in-one doll: a colonial mother and daughter outfitted with bonnets and shawls; a mother and her baby; two grannies; or twin babies joined with a bunting, one with a sleeping face and the other crying.

If you want one doll to disappear while the other is being played with, be sure to make the skirts long enough so that half the doll is always completely covered.

Soft-Sculpture Stocking Dolls

Dolls become most intriguing to me when their faces are developed into three-dimensional soft sculptures like those below and in the Craftnotes, opposite. Such faces delight both the youngest child and the most sophisticated adult, since they remind us of real people, not necessarily young and childlike but unforgettable characters nonetheless. In the Craftnotes, a technique is shown for sculpting a stuffed stocking head with needle and thread. Such sculpted heads can be stitched onto realistic bodies, like that of the lady on the locomotive, or on bodies that are merely suggested, like that of the engineer below and the sequined lady on page 1730. Or, if you prefer, you can make the head pillow-size and leave it at that.

E   **1 square = ½ inch**

Figure E: The two-in-one doll needs an extra-long torso, two waists, and two skirts, if it is to have correct proportions with either end up.

A little locomotion seems to be in order for this unusual couple. Such startling caricatures come not only from the soft sculpture technique described in the Craftnotes, but from a keen eye for detail.

CRAFTNOTES: MAKING SOFT-SCULPTURE FACES

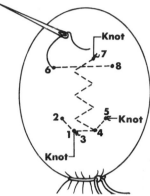

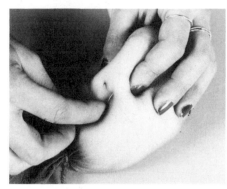

This old man's wrinkly, whiskery face was sculpted by the method described here. To make a three-dimensional face with needle and thread, first stuff a nylon stocking with cotton batting, polyester filling, or ideally, an old cotton undershirt, as was done with the old man.

Tie the stocking at the neck with yarn or cord. (Do not knot the stocking itself.)

Begin by forming a nostril. Pinch a shape for a nose with your fingers, as shown in the diagram above and in the photograph, above right. Knot the thread, and sew from point 1 to point 2, pulling on

the thread to make the shape; return the needle through points 2 and 1. To make the bridge between the nostrils, sew between points 3 and 4 and pull on the thread to shape. Form the other nostril by sewing between points 4 and 5, pull to shape, and secure the thread with a knot.

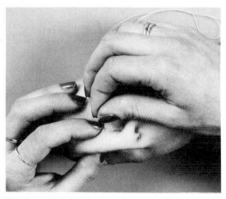

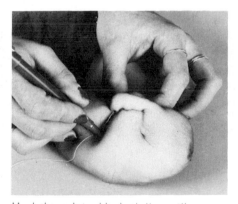

Pinch a nose bridge and secure the shape by sewing back and forth under it, approximately from point **4** to point **7**, and knot.

Pinch in the cheek contours.

Mark the points of indentation with a felt-tipped pen (above). Pull a thread between points 8 and 6 on the diagram to make eye sockets.

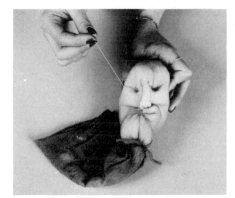

Sculpt cheeks by pulling a thread from the eye sockets to anywhere on the cheek area above.

Form an upper lip by pinching the shape (above) and bringing the stitch from the corners of the mouth to the outside nostril. This draws the fabric up to form an upper lip. Pinch a bottom lip with your fingers and take some stitches under it.

Complete the head by drawing or sewing on eyebrows, hair, even a mustache if you like. Accentuate wrinkles or lines with a felt-tipped pen. Sew beads into the eyes to give them sparkle (above).

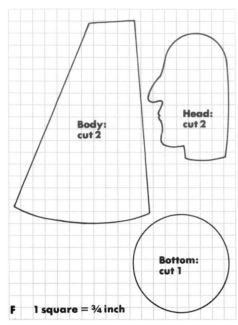

F 1 square = ¾ inch

Figure F: Enlarge these patterns by the method described in Figure D to make the free-form sequined doll at right. Vary the profile and body shapes to create the doll that most appeals to you.

Sequined Lady

Sculptural heads can also be created from profile patterns (Figure F) as was done for the sequined lady, below, and the giant doll, opposite, both sophisticated rag dolls made for adults. Patterns can be exaggerated caricatures or tracings of real-life silhouettes. Once such profile heads have been stitched and stuffed (the seam runs down the middle of the face), they can be sculpted further by the pulled-thread method described in the Craftnotes, page 1729. The cheeks of the glamorous sequined lady were accentuated by pulling a thread from the eye socket to the cheek on each side of the face. A thread pulled between the outside corners of the mouth created dimples. Dyes and tiny beads provide a glamorous finish for the face.

There is something chic about stepping out with rag dolls on your shoulder. The two-in-one doll on page 1728 inspired this carryall design.

Madam's free-form shape only suggests pale hands hidden beneath the sequins and furs. But her head with its arrogant tilt is carefully sculpted, tinted with dyes, and trimmed with brilliant beads.

Rag-Bag Doll

The rag dolls at left share body stuffing that comes and goes, depending on how much paraphernalia you put in or take out of the bag in the course of a day. A carry-all, it is derived from the traditional two-in-one doll on page 1728. The simple pattern (Figure G) can be cut in either two or four pieces, depending on how you want the sides of the bag to look. In the version pictured, two pieces of fabric, one brown and one white, were cut and pieced to form each side. To make a bag this way, cut four pieces, two of each color, and seam them as indicated in Figure H. When you have completed each side, stitch them together as depicted in Figure I. Stuff the sealed-off heads through the long arms, using a long-handled wooden spoon to pack the stuffing in. Then sew the two arms together to make a padded shoulder strap.

The top closing of the carryall can be a button and loop, a snap fastener, self-gripping tape, or a ribbon stitched around the middle and tied at the top. Create the doll faces with acrylic paints. Use yarn for hair and trim as you like with hand-stitched appliqués of ribbon and lace.

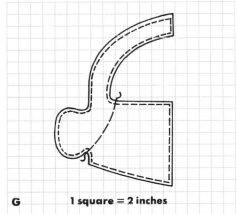

G   1 square = 2 inches

Figure G: Enlarge this pattern for the rag-doll carryall as described in Figure D, using a 2-inch grid. To make a side of two colors, as shown in the photograph, opposite, cut four side pieces. (To make a one-piece side, fold the fabric, place the straight edge of the pattern on the fold, pin, and cut.)

It is *la dolce vita* with this well-upholstered chair-person around to comfort and to cushion one after a hard day at the office.

Rag-Doll Furniture

If you take a rag doll to a larger-than-life extreme, you may have an enormous chair-person like exotic Gloria, above, to share your living room. She is as comfy to snuggle up with as she looks, since her torso is made from two ready-made pillows sewn together. Arms and legs, cut from strips of muslin and stuffed with cotton batting, were stitched onto the pillows. Her head was cut from a profile pattern, like that shown in Figure F, enlarged to larger than life-size. Antique boots from a thrift shop were stitched on for feet, and I sewed junk jewelry rings on her fingers. A black silk scarf stitched around her face and stuffed makes a very stylish pageboy bob. Her cigarette, by the way, is detachable, in case the hostess does not allow smoking. For related entries see "Animal Dolls," "Dolls and Doll Clothes."

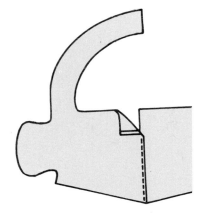

H

Figure H: Join the halves of each side of the carryall by folding under the seam allowance on one half and placing the folded edge along the seam line of the other half. Baste, then topstitch.

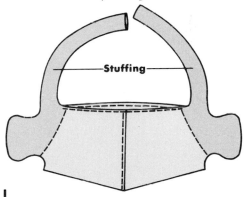

I

Figure I: Before joining the sides of the carryall, turn the seam allowance along the top opening inside, and stitch it down, reinforcing with bias tape at the corners. With right sides facing, join the sides, stitching around the bottom, heads, and arms, leaving the arms open at the wrists. Turn right side out, and topstitch the diagonal neck seams. Stuff the heads and arms through the arms; then join the ends of the arms, topstitching across the stuffing.

RECYCLING CLOTHES
From Sad Rags to Glad Rags

The urge to be creative is reason enough for many home sewers to recycle used clothing that others tend to store, give away, or scrap. Perhaps there is a special feeling of virtue that reclamation brings. Certainly there is enormous satisfaction in overcoming the limitations of an existing design to produce something fresh and new—converting pants into a skirt, applying decorative detailing, playing with color combinations, lengthening a dress by changing its proportions, adjusting the fit to accommodate a weight gain or loss, making the best of a bad bargain, salvaging a style that is too full, too narrow, or simply too obvious to suit current taste. Even so-called classics may be eclipsed by new versions with more timely fashion detailing.

Updating Outmoded Styles
Change is implicit in fashion up to a point. But at times, ready-to-wear designs change at a dizzying rate without apparent reason. In these circumstances, even the affluent must be sorely tempted to rescue good clothes from premature obsolescence. An actual need to cut clothing costs is, of course, an undeniable argument for recycling ready-to-wear clothes creatively.

Upwards of 45 million women and girls in the United States sew some of their clothes at home. What they make reflects different levels of experience, sophistication, talent, taste, and means. Their interest in sewing, however, reflects a shared desire to make use of their skills, whether by choice or of necessity. As clothing needs and individual tastes become more varied, and as leisure time increases, home sewing will continue to grow. Recycling is part of that art.

Leah Chatt Berger worked in the fashion industry as a designer after graduation from the Fashion Institute of Technology in New York. She holds a degree in home economics and a minor in fine arts from the University of North Carolina at Greensboro. Among friends and neighbors in Harrington Park, New Jersey, Leah is known as a clothing doctor. She spends her free time sculpting, painting, teaching stained-glass design, and studying carpentry at a studio in Manhattan.

Needlecrafts
Workday blues with dash

You can transform old jeans or any pair of pants into an A-line skirt by opening the inside leg and crotch seams and setting in triangular godets.

Two separate sad rags, boy's jeans and a washed-out cotton-knit top, were recycled into a coordinated costume for a teen-age girl.

Cotton-knit shirts of good quality can be recycled. It also pays to salvage nearly new ones that have met with some slight mishap.

Opposite: Don't throw away that old garment hanging in your closet; recycle it. You can change the style, alter the fit, and add decorative detailing. Projects that follow will show you how.

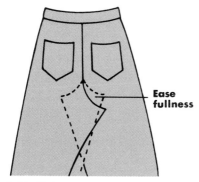

1: Before inserting the triangular godets that will turn pants into an A-line skirt, overlap the crotch flaps until they lie smoothly, and pin them in place front and back. With this step, the silhouette changes.

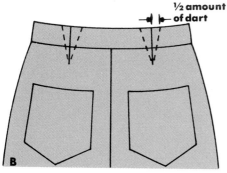

Ease fullness

A
Figure A: To eliminate excessive fullness at the back of a jeanskirt, lift the overlapping flap of the crotch towards the waist.

½ amount of dart

B
Figure B: To make the waistline smaller, make darts by folding the excess fabric inside and stitching on both sides of the dart from the waistband as far down into the skirt as necessary.

Jeans into Skirt

The boy's worn jeans reclaimed as a skirt, pictured on page 1733, are a good introduction to the process of remodeling. The technique for making a skirt out of pants applies to any fabric—linen, gabardine, crepe, satin, velvet, and brocade, to cite a few examples—as readily as it does to denim. If you have gained weight, a skirt provides more room than pants. After the inside leg seams are opened, the straight side line becomes an A line and triangular insets, called godets, are sewn into the center front and back. Some projects that seem complicated are really elementary—this is one of them.

Making Godets

To make godets for a long skirt, you will need either an extra yard of fabric or a second pair of jeans that are at least 14 inches in circumference at the bottom of each leg. Such opened leg sections provide enough material. Alternatively, godets can be cut from striped ticking or a cotton flower print. If you choose to make a short skirt out of jeans, use the legs of that same pair for the godets—there will be enough fabric.

To convert pants into a skirt, first open the inside leg seams and crotch seams up to the bottom of the zipper in front and up to the point in the back where the crotch pieces can be overlapped so they lie flat. Next, take the extra yard of godet fabric, fold it in half, and cut it down the center to obtain two equal rectangles. Overlap the crotch pieces, following the direction of the front flap closing, until the fabric lies smooth (photograph 1). Pin, then baste the overlap into place, back and front. If there is too much fullness in the seat, lift the back overlap of the crotch toward the waist. Pin to hold it at the desired point; then baste the overlap into place, easing in the excess fullness as you baste (Figure A). Place the jeans flat, right side up. Place a rectangle of the fabric to be added, face up, under the open triangle at the center front of the jeans. Pin and baste the godet into place.

Topstitching

Next, use topstitching to join the pieces permanently. Topstitching has two functions: it holds the seams flat, and it accents them neatly. Such stitching can be done with contrasting thread or with matching thread, depending on the effect you want. It is done on the right side of the garment, so the stitching must be straight and even. Topstitch close to the edge and cover the original line of stitching. Topstitch the seam that runs under the crotch flap first, running the stitches about ¼ inch under and beyond the overlap. Topstitch a second row ¼ inch to ⅜ inch in from the edge, following the original line if there is one. Next, topstitch the crotch overlap and the second side of the inset using a double row of stitches. Finally, turn the skirt inside out, and cut away the excess fabric from godet and crotch areas, cutting about ¼ inch from the seams. Insert the rear godet the same way.

Fitting the Waist with Darts

If the skirt is too large at the waist, use triangular tucks, called darts, to make it fit. You can dart from the waistline as far down as necessary (Figure B), but the dart must go below the waistline seam to keep the fabric in the skirt from puckering. The best locations for new darts are in the back, about 3½ inches on each side of the center. You can dart the waistline at the same places in front as well, if you need to. Try on the skirt. Pinch in the excess fabric, thus forming the darts, and pin them in place. Take off the skirt and lay it flat. On the inside of the skirt, mark each dart with chalk along the pin lines, which will be the stitching lines. Remove the pins, and draw a third chalk line down the center to indicate the fold line. As a further guide, draw a chalk line at a right angle to the point of the dart and a parallel line halfway up so you can match these points when you repinch and repin the dart, moving it to the wrong side for sewing. Stitch the darts from the waistline down to the end point.

Darts are usually pressed flat, either to the left or the right side of the seam, so the garment looks smooth on the outside. When the fabric is as heavy as denim, you can take off the waistband to avoid sewing through the extra thicknesses of fabric; or you can avoid the extra work and still get a smooth waistline by slashing the finished darts down the center and pressing them open. Trim the dart first, allowing a ⅜-inch seam as far down as possible. Then slash the fold to within ½ inch from the point. Press along the stitching line, then on each side.

To add a finishing touch to your jeanskirt, cover any worn sections in the jeans with patches, and decorate them with nailheads.

Coordinated Knit Top

A faded blue cotton-knit boy's shirt became a favorite coordinate for a girl's faded jeanskirt (page 1733) after some creative recycling. My preference for a garment that would slip over the head easily inspired the open V-shaped neckline. Then came the idea of facing the neckline on the right side of the fabric as a base for the decorative nailhead border which coordinates the shirt with the skirt. I adapted a commercial pattern with a squared armhole and a high, round neckline. The long sleeves of the shirt were removed, providing material for the armhole and neckline facings. I extended the front facing down into a bib shape to accommodate the open neckline (Figure C). Any shirt that starts with a round neckline and long, set-in sleeves can be restyled the same way and trimmed as you like.

First, take out the neckband and the sleeves. Fold each sleeve in half lengthwise, and use it as the source of fabric for facings. One sleeve provides the neckline facing, the other the armhole facings (Figure C). Lay out the front and back neckline facings along the fold of one sleeve, but position the front piece high enough so you can add on the biblike extension (dashed line, Figure C). Cut the facings as close to the straight grain as possible, including the bib in the front facing. Follow the commercial pattern in cutting the armhole facings from the second sleeve.

Try on the shirt to check the fit. If the shoulder seam extends too far out, as this one did, mark it with chalk or with a pin at the point where the armhole should end, as a guide in attaching the armhole facings. Like all boys' shirts, this one was too square for a girl's figure. It had to be shaped to an easy fit by pinning it along the side seams. Even a boxy style will need some adjusting because a cotton knit loses its shape with wear. Mark the bottom at the desired length. Take off the shirt, and sew the new side seams on the inside.

Now you are ready to attach the neckline facing. With right sides together, stitch both shoulder seams that join the two pieces of the neckline facing. Place the biblike front facing, wrong side up, on the wrong side of the shirt front, smoothing it as you pin it in place all around its edge. Follow the line of the facing rather than neckline of the shirt, should there be a discrepancy, because the shirt fabric may be stretched.

Making a V-shaped Neckline

Here, I decided to make a V-shaped neckline open 2½ inches at the top and 5 inches deep. This is how to do it. To find the center front of the inside-out garment, fold it in half, matching the shoulders. Mark the center front of the facing at the top; then measure 5½ inches down along the fold and mark again. The extra ½ inch is the seam allowance. Open the shirt flat. Rule a line to connect the dots (Figure D). To create an opening 2½ inches wide on top, measure 1¼ inches out from the vertical line in both directions. Draw the V shape with a ruler. Sew all around the neckline opening, joining the facing to the shirt at the garment's edge. Trim closely along this seam. Turn the shirt right side out; open the seam and press flat.

With the front facing now right side up on the right side of the shirt, topstitch the neckline close to the edge. Topstitch a second row ¼ inch inside the first (Figure E). The finished band is 1½ inches wide, but I added a ½-inch seam allowance along the inner edge before cutting off the excess fabric. This edge of the band is now turned under and topstitched in place, again with a double row of stitching. The same kind of topstitching is used around the armholes (faced using the commercial pattern) and around the bottom of the shirt.

I decorated the neckband with nailheads in two sizes by pushing the spiked ends through the fabric and pressing down the points with a scrap of wood.

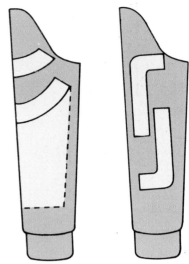

C
Figure C: When you remodel a shirt, cut neckline facings from one of the long sleeves that you removed, armhole facings from the other. The neckline facings are lined up along the fold; the dotted line indicates the biblike extension on the front facing which permits a V-shaped neckline.

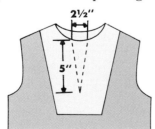

D
Figure D: To create an opening 2½ inches wide at the top of the neckline, measure 1¼ inches out from the vertical line in the center to a point 5 inches down. Draw a V shape with ruler and chalk.

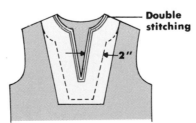

E
Figure E: Two rows of topstitching, one at the outer edge, the other ¼ inch in, decorate a neckline which has been faced on the right side of the fabric. The inner edge of the facing is to be turned under and topstitched.

Needlecrafts
Glad raglan two-top

¢ 🗙 🚶 🪡

One for the price of two may be a bargain if the alternative is zero; so I combined two nearly new cotton-knit boy's shirts that had run afoul of chemicals during photo developing. They were permanently stained on the outside, but the wrong sides were still perfect; so I turned the shirt inside out. I used the blue body and the yellow sleeves to make a shirt for a girl.

Remove all four sleeves by opening the stitches. Do not cut the sleeves—the amount you snip off may be just what you need later on. Let the neckband remain on the body piece as a temporary anchor while you try on the shirt or fit it on somebody else. Using pins, shape it to an easy fit, and mark the length. Take off the shirt, remove neckband and pockets, and run up the side seams with a **zigzag** stitch (see Craftnotes—a straight stitch might break when the shirt is pulled over the head or it might make the fabric pucker.)

CRAFTNOTES:

Recycle the easy way

Your equipment is the same when you recycle clothes as when you do any other sewing. Besides the sewing machine, work table, iron and ironing board, you need: scissors; a seam ripper; a measuring tape; thimble; pins; needles; marking chalk; a see-through ruler; and a yardstick.

Use a medium needle and polyester thread for all sewing except when you are inserting elastic; then use elastic thread on the bobbin, but do not change the top thread.

Use commercial patterns for details. Fabrics that are no longer new (knits in particular) may have stretched out of shape, but you can control the accuracy of line on details such as necklines, armholes, and facings by using a commercial pattern instead of trying to work freehand. Using a pattern will speed the work, too.

Neckline facings can be decorative as well as functional. In general, neckline facings are stitched together at the shoulder seams before being sewn to the neck edge of the garment. Use the pattern piece of the facing as a guide in cutting when you want to interface. The interfacing is a third layer of fabric that is sandwiched between a garment fabric and a facing to reinforce the shape or to provide crispness.

Remove stitches carefully. Use a seam ripper or a small, sharp scissors. Cut stitches at 1-inch intervals on one side of the seamline, and pull out the thread on the opposite side. Never pull the edges apart.

Pin, then baste with a very long running stitch (about 1 inch long), either by hand or by machine, whenever there is question of fit. Always baste when fitting an inside curve to an outside curve, as when setting in a sleeve. Baste when making darts to fit and also when working with more than two layers of fabric.

Working with knits

Working with stretchy cotton knits calls for extra care. Stitch them with threads of polyester, cotton-covered polyester, or nylon because they are flexible enough to give with the knit. It is the stitch, rather than the thread, however, that may cause puckering in knits when they are being sewn or may break when the garment is pulled over the head.

If you own a zigzag machine, use a narrow, closely spaced zigzag stitch when you sew knits. But test the tension—it may need to be loosened. The correct adjustment gives you a balanced stitch that is identical on both sides of the fabric (see drawings at right, opposite). As a rule, only the upper thread tension needs to be set. The edges of jersey knits will not ravel, but they may tend to curl under. If they do, use a zigzag stitch on the edges of facings and to finish the seams. With a straight-stitch machine, you can incorporate some stretch into knits. Hold the fabric, one hand in front, and stretch it gently while you are sewing.

About stitches

There are two basic types of machine stitching: straight and zigzag. With straight stitching, the length of the stitch and the tension of the thread can be adjusted. With a zigzag stitch, the length and width of the stitch as well as the thread tension are adjustable. Check your sewing machine manual for instructions on how to adjust these variables. In straight stitching, the sewing machine needle moves up and down only, stitching in a continuous line. In the basic zigzag stitch, the sewing machine needle moves from side to side as it moves forward.

Construction stitches

Stitches for general clothes construction are usually 10 to 15 stitches to the inch. The lighter the weight of the fabric, the shorter the stitch.

Machine baste and baste stitch are terms used interchangeably to denote basting stitches which are long because they are only temporary.

Gathering stitches consist of two rows of long basting stitches. They are used to gather the fabric along the lines of stitching, which can be done by pulling the bobbin thread.

Ease stitching is used to ease in an edge with extra fullness to fit another, shorter edge. There are generally eight to ten stitches to the inch.

Stay stitching is a line of machine stitching. It is made inside a seam allowance before construction stitching to prevent curved or bias edges from stretching out of shape.

Edge stitching refers to a line of stitching placed close to an edge, either finished or turned under. If the stitching is done on the outside of the garment, it is called topstitching. Guidelines on the throat plate of the

Old, stained T-shirts of the same style can be salvaged by combining them, turning them inside out and using the good parts of each.

Two shirts with raglan sleeves have been recycled into one that is a standout. The bi-color knit makes an attractive top to wear with jeans.

SEWING TIPS

machine or even a piece of adhesive tape placed at the desired distance from the presser foot will help you achieve a perfectly straight line of stitching.

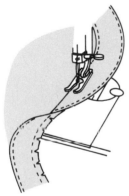

Understitching (above) is a row of stitching made close to the edge of a faced seam on the right side of the facing to hold the facing in place and make the seam edge more precise.

Reinforcement stitches, about 18 or 20 to the inch, are very small to provide extra holding power at points of stress—a corner, a point to be trimmed and turned, or an inside curve that will be clipped.

Decorative stitches

The basic zigzag stitch makes possible a variety of saw-tooth effects by adjusting the width (side-to-side measurement) and length (spacing between stitches). It can also be used as a construction stitch when working with knits.

The satin stitch, a machine embroidery stitch used to appliqué, is made with zigzag stitches compressed to nearly zero length.

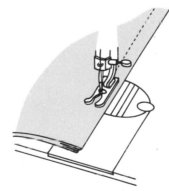

Topstitching, visible on the right side of the garment, is decorative as well as functional. Edges that have been turned under and topstitched do away with the need for facings on necklines and armholes. In double topstitching, one row lies close to the edge, and the second row runs in a parallel line.

Thread tension

A stitch should be balanced identically on both sides of the fabric to avoid puckering or loose thread. Check the manual for the suggested tension setting. Usually only the needle thread (upper thread) needs adjustment. Bobbin tension is set at the factory and should not need to be reset. If it does, have the job done by a professional repairman.

If the upper thread tension is too loose (or the lower thread tension too tight), thread will lie stretched out on the underside of the fabric, as above.

When the tension of the upper thread is too tight (or the lower thread too loose), the thread lies stretched on the top of the fabric.

When tensions are properly adjusted and in balance, the threads are drawn equally into the fabric, and stitches look alike on both sides.

Machine-gather the front raglan armholes of the blue body and of the yellow raglan sleeves, using the largest straight stitch on your machine (photograph 2). Before stitching, loosen the needle tension enough to let you pull the bobbin thread freely. Ease in the fullness about 1 inch on both sleeves and armholes. Make a row of stitches a presser foot away from the edge, and knot the threads at one end. At the other end, pull the bobbin thread carefully, and push the material along this thread until the fabric is the correct length. Then knot the bobbin and top threads together. Press the sleeves and the armholes smooth. Set in both sleeves, pinning as you match seams at underarm and along raglan line, and stitch them into place (photograph 3). If there is extra fabric at the edge, ignore it for the moment because you must try on the garment again at this point to determine how long you want the shirt and the sleeves to be and how low you want the neckline.

Making the Neckline

The neckline of the shirt pictured (page 1737) is just high enough on the shoulders to conceal the bra straps. I used pins to establish the neckline, front and back. If you can't manage to mark the back yourself, ask someone to help. Take off the shirt and lay it flat. Use a ruler and chalk or pencil to mark your neckline cutting guideline, which should provide a ⅝-inch seam allowance (photograph 4). Open the raglan seams, front and back, down to the marked neckline. Turn under and pin the front (photograph 5), the back, and tops of the sleeves so that the lines are straight (photograph 6). Zigzag stitching in reverse colors emphasizes the two-color design. This stitching is sewn ⅜ inch in from the edge (photograph 7). Only the pocket, placed as close to the hem as possible for a boutique touch, is straight stitched with matching yellow thread.

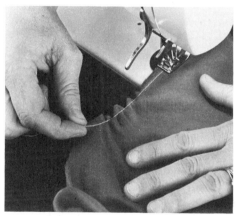

2: Gather a raglan armhole to ease in the extra fullness. Adjust the sleeve in the same way, using ⅛-inch running stitches on the machine.

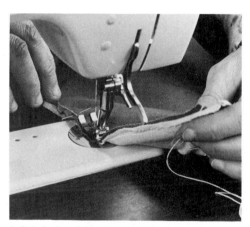

3: Stitch the raglan sleeve into its armhole, matching the sleeve seam with the underarm seam of the shirt.

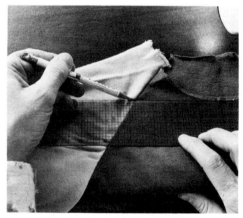

4: Place a ruler across the front of the shirt, touching the center point of the new neckline, and mark the point where it reaches the raglan seams.

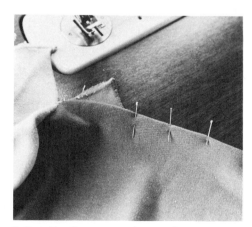

5: Open the sleeve seams down to the markings, fold under, and pin the front of the shirt in a straight line. Then do the same with the back.

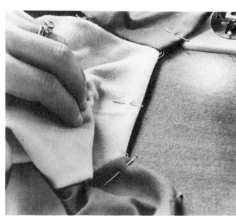

6: Fold back the tops of the sleeves in the same way, and pin them to establish the rectangular shapes at the shoulders.

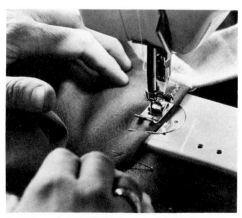

7: Yellow zigzag stitching on the blue body, and blue stitching on the yellow sleeves, complete a harmonious contrast.

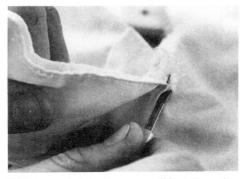

8: The man-styled collar comes off first. Open the stitches carefully with a seam ripper or small scissors so the fabric does not tear—never rip a seam open.

This man-tailored classic shirt was restyled into a short, colorful shirt to wear with jeans.

Stripped of all its telltale shirt markings, a familiar classic is transformed into a casual top.

Needlecrafts
A camouflaged classic   ¢ ⊠ ♣ 🐚

There are many ways to disguise a man-tailored shirt when you have one too many in your closet. The one above, left, was decollared, desleeved, shortened, nipped in at the waist with elastic thread, and trimmed with orange braid. When you remove the collar (photograph 8), you will discover a mandarin neckband ready to be accentuated. Adjust the band so it is the same width all around by measuring the narrowest portion (at the center front) and using it as your guide (photograph 9). Turn under each side of the opened seam, and baste the two sides together. Place the braid trimming along the pinned edge, and sew all three layers together (photograph 10). Sew a parallel row of trimming at the bottom of the neckband and repeat the decoration on the front closing. Try on the shirt to establish the length you want, and hem it up with orange thread.

An easy way to fit a shirt is to elasticize the waistline at several points (or all the way around if there is considerable material to blouse). I used elastic thread (available in any notions department) as the bobbin thread and kept the tension fairly tight. The upper thread need not be changed but I used orange to match the trimming on the blouse. However, use the largest stitch on your machine in order to give the elastic thread sufficient play. Stitch as many parallel rows as you wish, ¼ inch apart, using the presser foot as a guide.

To transform long shirt-sleeves into short cuffed ones, cut them at the elbow (Figure F). Fold the raw edge under 3½ inches and hem. The stitching will not be visible after the cuff has been turned up. Stitch trimming to the inner edge of the cuff so it will be on the right side when the cuff is turned up.

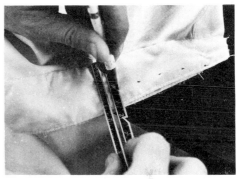

9: The makings of a mandarin neckline lie under the collar. Mark it so it will be the same width all around; measure the width at the center front and use that as your guide.

10: Braid is sewn on at the same time as the pinned edge of the mandarin neckline is stitched.

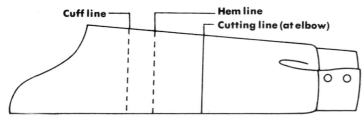

Figure F: Convert long shirt-sleeves into short cuffed ones by cutting them near the elbow. Fold them under and up about 3½ inches, and hem. The turned-back cuffs hide the stitches.

1739

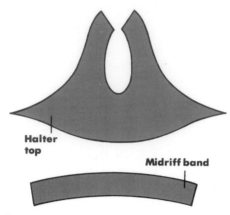

Halter top

Midriff band

G

Figure G: There is sufficient print material in the cummerbund for the halter top plus a 14¾-inch-long piece to use on the front of the halter's midriff band.

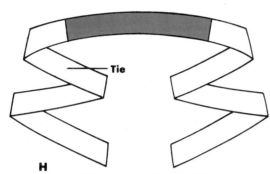

Tie

H

Figure H: The linings of the midriff piece and the halter ties are cut out of white fabric, the background color of the print material, and are seamed together.

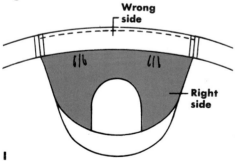

Wrong side

Right side

I

Figure I: With right sides facing, stitch the front of the midriff band to the halter top.

The long print skirt with its matching cummerbund was attractive, but no blouse seemed to look right with it.

The halter, cut from the cummerbund, has a wrap-and-tie midriff section that combines print fabric with white, connecting visually to the skirt.

Needlecrafts
Halter it the same   ¢ ☒ 🚶 🪡

There are some printed skirts, attractive in themselves, that somehow do not appear to belong with any sort of contrasting top. The skirt above, left, falls into this category, providing a reason for recycling the cummerbund into a halter.

Opened and pressed flat, the cummerbund measured 16 by 30 inches—sufficient material to make a bare-midriff halter top but not enough to make the waist-length model preferred. The scant amount of matching print raised the question of how to carry through a border effect from halter to skirt without apparent interruption. The solution required an additional 1 yard of fabric 45 inches wide, commercial pattern pieces for a halter bodice with a set-in midriff band, and determination to salvage every scrap of print. By making a print halter out of the cummerbund and lining it with the white background color, it is possible to create a means of linking the top with the skirt.

Cut both layers of the halter top. With right sides facing, stitch the print and the white sections together around the neckline and sides; then turn the top right side out and press. Stitch the seam at the center back of the neck by hand. Try on the halter to adjust the fit under the bustline. Hold in excess fabric with pins. Take off the top, and machine-gather the halter under the bustline, following the directions on page 1742.

The midriff pattern was for a band 2¾ inches wide excluding the ⅝-inch seam allowances (Figure G). From the scraps of print left over after cutting out the halter top, choose a piece large enough (4¼ by 14¾ inches) to form a center front panel for the midriff band. Cut a piece of white fabric the same size to line the print. Then cut four layers of white fabric to make the two streamer ties. Each white piece is 4¼ by 41¾ inches, including a ⅝-inch seam allowance.

Join the three front sections, placing the print between the two white sections. Then join the three lining sections, all white (Figure H). With right sides facing, sew along all sides, leaving only the top of the center section open. Turn right side out. With right sides facing, join the center of the print midriff section to the center front of the halter, and stitch (Figure I). Fold under the seam allowance on the reverse (white) side of the band, and stitch it to the halter by hand.

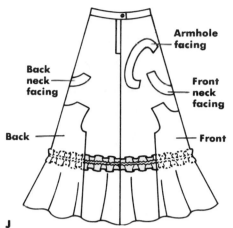

This woman's skirt was recycled into a child's dress in such a way that the ruffle and the original hem could be incorporated without change.

This child's dress was made from the yellow skirt at the left. It contains, in miniature but intact, original design features.

Figure J: Place pieces from a commercial pattern for a child's dress on top of a woman's skirt in such a way that you can take advantage of the flounced hemline and trimming.

Needlecrafts
Appliquéd dress for a child   ¢ ⊠ ⚹ 🔥

A once-cherished skirt of sturdy cotton denim (above, left), had such obvious detailing that everyone grew tired of it. Still as good as new, it had nowhere to go except into mothballs for a few years or into the recycling bin. It was recycled, much altered, as a dress for a five-year-old. Once I decided how to take advantage of the good features—the finished flounce hemline and the gingham ruffle—I was able to make the conversion in about three hours. Although clothes with decorative design features are a challenge to home sewers, the built-in trimmings can be a bonus. You probably do not own a skirt exactly like this, but you may have another with flounces or ruffles that you can use.

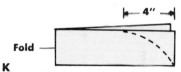

11: A very close zigzag stitch (also called a satin stitch) is used to appliqué a gingham heart onto the dress.

Use a Commercial Pattern
After you remove the waistband and zipper from the skirt, fold it so a side seam is at the center of the front, and place it flat on the table. Use a commercial pattern for cutting out the child's dress. Place all the pieces on the skirt as diagramed in Figure J, and pin them down. The front and back pieces of the dress are flush with the bottom of the skirt to take advantage of the finished hemline. Both are positioned along side folds. If your skirt has one seam in the center of the front, place the front pattern piece on this seam. After you have cut out the pieces, pin and sew the skirt zipper into the center of the back section of the dress.

Figure K: To cut a pair of cap sleeves with symmetrical curves, fold each piece lengthwise, and mark a curved cutting guideline about 4 inches long on the diagonal.

Do the heart appliqué next. I cut out a 2¾-by-3-inch paper heart to fit the width of the gingham left over from the ruffle. I pressed the ruffle flat, cut out two hearts, pinned them respectively into position, and basted them to the bodice. The satin stitch, a very close zigzag stitch, is used to appliqué (photograph 11). Adjust your machine, setting the stitch-length regulator close to zero so the stitches lie close to each other. Go around the edge twice if you want heavier definition. Remove the basting stitches when you are finished.

Stitch the neck-facing pieces together at the shoulder seams. Turn under ¼ inch of the outer edge to the wrong side of the facing, and stitch all around for a clean finish. With the right sides of dress and facing together and shoulder seams matching, stitch around the neckline. Trim and notch the seams until the facing is smooth. Now understitch the neckline edge (see Craftnotes, page 1736-1737) so the facing will remain flat: open the facing out flat, with the neck seam margins following in the direction of the facing, and stitch close to the facing seam on the right side of the facing. At the back zipper, turn the facing to the inside and stitch down by hand.

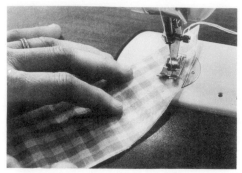

12: The curved raw edge of the shoulder ruffle for the child's dress (page 1741) is machine-gathered by using the largest stitch on the machine.

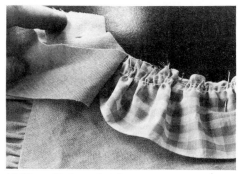

13: To make a ruffle, pull the bobbin threads (on the bottom) of each row of stitching until the ruffle is half its original length.

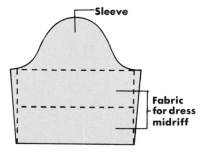

14: The ruffle is sandwiched between the facing (left) and the armhole which have been placed with the right sides together.

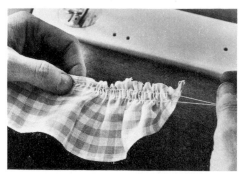

L
Figure L: Cuffed sleeves, opened and pressed, provide enough material to make the front and back of a midriff band used to lengthen a dress.

Press and use the remaining pieces of ruffle left over from the skirt to make the ruffled cap sleeves. I was able to get a length of 15 inches for each sleeve, but 13 inches will do. Fold each of the two gingham pieces in half lengthwise; place one on top of the other and match the folds, then mark one curved cutting guideline on the top layer (Figure K, page 1741). This will assure perfect symmetry at the curved ends when you cut both sleeves at the same time. The curved cutting guidelines should measure about 4 inches on the diagonal from one end to the other.

Machine gather the curved side until it is only 7½ inches long, using the largest straight stitch on your machine. Sew the first row ¼ inch in from the edge (photograph 12) and the second row a presser foot away; then pull the bobbin threads (photograph 13). The gingham ruffle already had a hem on the edge. If there were none, I would have hemmed it by hand.

Before attaching the ruffle, fold it in half to find the center. With right sides facing, pin the center to the armhole at the end of the shoulder seam; then pin down completely. Make a ¼-inch hem on the armhole facing. Pin the facing to the armhole, right sides together, with the ruffle sandwiched between (photograph 14). Sew, trim the seam, and turn facing to the inside. Sew the armhole facing and the side seam of the dress together. Be sure to enclose the edge of the gingham in the seam. Stitch down the armhole facing by hand.

Needlecrafts
Lengthening a dress

Some of the basic dresses that I have accumulated over the years are too short to suit me now. The yellow dress, pictured opposite, was one of them. Besides being short, it bunched around the middle in an unattractive manner, producing a squared-off look. Although it was a shift style, a band of elastic had been sewn inside the waistline. This shaping device might have worked with a thin, supple fabric such as crepe, but it was not successful with heavy linen which happened to be reversible.

My plan was to fit the bodice as well as lengthen the dress. I was able to accomplish both simultaneously by snipping out the elastic and setting in a fitted band 2 inches wide directly under the bust. I left the skirt alone. The sleeves provided enough fabric for the empire-style inset. If I were a larger size, or if I had wished to insert bands in the skirt as well, I would have needed extra fabric and would have used the same white fabric I chose for the collar. Any shift of this type can be lengthened from the bodice.

Remove the cuffed sleeves, open them and press them flat, as shown in Figure L. One sleeve provides material for the front of the inset band, the other for the back. Press the dress and slip into it. Position a tape measure as shown in Figure M around your rib cage to establish where the top of the new band will be joined to the bodice. The actual cut-off line is at the bottom of the tape because the distance between the top and bottom of the tape automatically provides a ⅝-inch seam allowance. Mark the bottom with chalk (you may need help with marking the back).

Fold and Cut Off Bodice
Take off the dress. Fold and pin it from center front to back with armholes matched, as shown in Figure N, and cut off the bodice. Try the bodice on again in order to dart it, front and back, so it fits under the bust. Front darts are centered under the bust. Back darts are placed on each side about 3 inches from the middle. Again, you will need help to pin the darts in the back. Follow directions on page 1734 for making darts. Take in the underarm seams to compensate for the removal of the sleeves.

The width of the finished band is 2 inches, but initially the band pieces are 4¼ inches wide to accommodate the ⅝-inch seam allowances top and bottom, plus 1 inch more for shaping the band to the natural curve of the diaphragm.

Cut the four band pieces from the sleeves. For the front pieces, measure the distance across the bodice from the center to the side seam, add 2 inches to each piece (so that you can turn it under the front closing later), and cut.

Then measure the distance across the back of the bodice, allowing ⅝ inch each for seams in the center of the back and at the sides. Cut two band pieces of equal length to fit. Now you are ready to curve the band (Figure O).

A woman's dress, too short, and too square through the midsection to be comfortable, was re-styled with the help of a fitted midriff band.

A set-in midriff, made from the sleeves of the original dress (left), lengthens and shapes the recycled version without appearing contrived.

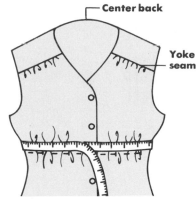

Figure M: A tape measure circling the midriff below the bust is pinned in place and marked with chalk at the bottom to indicate the cut-off line where the bodice will be separated from the skirt. The width of the tape provides a ⅝-inch seam allowance. The collar to be added will extend down to the yoke lines in front.

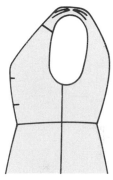

Figure N: To establish a symmetrical line for cutting the bodice from the skirt, fold the dress from the center front to the center back and pin it so the armholes match.

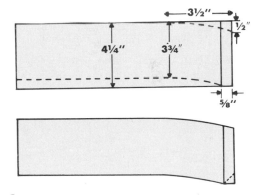

Figure O: The midriff band needs to be shaped to conform to the natural curve of the diaphragm. Stack the four pieces, right side up, with the side seam allowance at the right end. Measure ½ inch down from the top, at the seam allowance line, and chalk a curved line from the outer edge to a point that will correspond with the bustline dart (about 3½ inches in from the side). Mark the adjusted width of 3¾ inches along the bottom edge by measuring down from the top (top drawing). Cut off the excess fabric, top and bottom, and at an angle from the side seam allowance (bottom drawing). Then sew the band pieces together.

Place the four band pieces on top of each other so the four side ends are lined up on your right. If your fabric is not reversible, arrange the pieces in pairs, right sides together. With ruler and chalk, measure in to a point ⅝ inch from the side ends, and draw a line. Measure ½ inch down from the top of the band, and mark the point of intersection. This point falls directly under the arms. Make another dot about 3½ inches in from the side. This point should be centered directly under the bust dart in front. Draw a curved line between the two points, extending it out to the end of the seam allowance. Cut the top curve in all four band pieces. Measure the same distance down from the top of the band at intervals all along its length, and connect the dots. This will give you the bottom curve. Cut the curve, and angle the seam allowance up from the bottom (as shown in Figure O, bottom); then sew the band sections together. Baste the top of the band to the bodice, matching center back and side seams. Gather the top of the skirt to fit the band, pin it, and baste it to the bottom of the band, matching the seams. Topstitch ¼ inch from the edge all around the band, top and bottom. Turn the ends at the front opening underneath, and hem them by hand. I used commercial patterns for the armhole facing (which I finished in a conventional manner) and for the wide, white collar.

Making the Collar

The collar that was added to the dress stops at the front shoulder yoke, as I had planned (Figure M). But the pattern piece for it had to be adjusted in length to correspond with the dress neckline, from the center back to the yoke line. The pattern was 1 inch too long; so I folded it back and pinned it at the shoulder marking. If the pattern had fallen short of the yoke, I would have added the extra length by cutting at the shoulder markings, fitting a piece of tissue between the cut sections, and taping them together. In sewing two pieces of the collar, right sides facing, leave the bottom open. Trim the seams, turn the collar right side out, press, and topstitch the bottom ¼ inch from the edge. Bind this edge with bias tape so the collar is removable. Sew the collar onto the neckline by hand. Trim it with braid, stitching the braid on by hand or machine, ⅜ inch in from the edge.

For related entries, see "Fur Recycling" and "Sewing without a Pattern."

REPOUSSÉ AND CHASED METAL
Tooling Embossed Designs

Marianne Sabados Benedikt and her husband, Michael, a poet, live in New York with their six cats. Marianne's interest in embossing metal grew out of her work with jewelry designs. She holds masters' degrees in both art education and library service.

Sheets of gold, silver, and less precious metals have been decorated with hammers and chisels for thousands of years. To adorn both useful and ceremonial objects, primitive craftsmen hammered square- or round-edged tools into the back of the metal, thus raising a design on the front. This is repoussé. To further define and embellish the design, the metal was then turned right side up and its surface was worked with narrow, tapered tools. This is chasing. These complementary techniques were used by the Coclé Indians of Panama about 1200 A.D. to decorate the gold plate shown opposite; the processes used by today's craftsmen (below, opposite) are essentially the same.

The projects that follow will introduce you to the techniques used in embossing metal. Exercised in their simplest form, repoussé and chasing work can be done with pointed or rounded wooden modeling tools. Pressed into a thin sheet of metal, these tools can create an elaborate gift box (page 1747) or a mirror or picture frame (page 1749). More advanced techniques, used to emboss thicker metal such as the sterling silver necklace (page 1751), are harder to master. The metal must be supported by a surface of precisely the right resiliency as it is shaped with forged steel chisels.

For embossing sheet metal, you will need tools for impressing shapes in it and two work surfaces, one hard and one resilient. For repoussé, you will need a surface with a fair amount of give to it so the front of the metal is not marred as the design is raised. A felt or rubber pad, carpet remnant, or stack of newspapers will serve. For chasing, you will need a hard smooth surface such as tempered hardboard or glass. Sheet metal is available at craft shops and jewelry supply houses in a variety of gauges—the higher the gauge number, the thinner the metal. Although gold and silver are frequently used, aluminum, copper, pewter, bronze, and brass are equally suitable and considerably less expensive. Tools needed are listed separately with each project.

Basic Techniques

In impressing designs in thin sheet metal, the procedure is to alternate between repoussé and chasing, and to repeat each step several times. This is done chiefly because thin sheet metal is so fragile that if you attempt to emboss it deeply all at once you are likely to rip through it. If the final design calls only for low relief, you may be able to press the raised areas to about half their final height in the first round of repoussé work. As you push on the metal to create raised areas, it will stretch, resulting in a certain amount of distortion. Once you have pressed all raised areas to approximately the same height, turn the piece over and chase the front to define the outline of each design and to eliminate any distortion. Then turn the metal back for the second round of repoussé and chasing. Repeat these steps until the relief areas are at the height desired without any distortion.

Even with thin metal it is hard to keep the surface smooth between raised designs. That is why you need a hard work surface for chasing—you don't want a raised design on both sides.

Be cautious as you pull an embossing tool across the metal—work in a uniform direction with an even, flowing motion. I find that the hardest design to scribe on a slippery metal surface is a straight line because the metal tends to resist the tool at unexpected moments. Before you begin a project, experiment with different embossing tools on scrap metal to determine how much resistance it offers. And as you plan your own designs, avoid patterns with many closely spaced lines.

Rounded and straight-edged tools were used by the Coclé Indians of Panama to emboss the 7-by-10-inch gold plaque opposite (top). This symmetrical pattern was created some 700 years ago. Similar techniques were used by a contemporary craftsman, Gianmaria Buccellati, to make the sterling silver tray opposite (lower right). A detail (lower left) shows the complexity of this work.

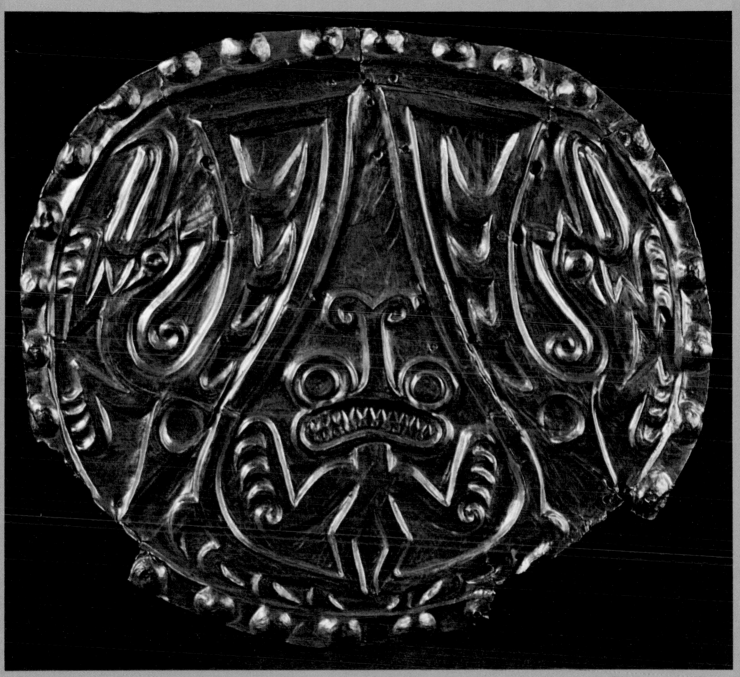

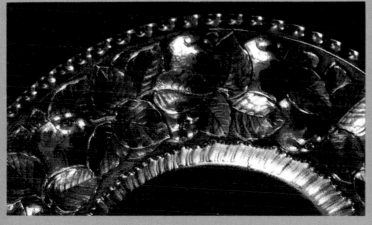

Ornamented box tops

A thin sheet of copper, embossed with a design inspired by a fabric from the island of Mali, was used to wrap the cardboard gift box shown opposite. But other motifs, such as the frog design (Figure B), are equally suitable. You can transfer almost any design that appeals to you onto the top of a box that you will use for a special gift or for storing keepsakes and jewelry.

To cover a small cardboard gift box with embossed metal you will need: a sheet of 40-gauge copper or aluminum; sharp scissors; 8-by-10-inch sheets of tracing paper; ruler; pencil or empty ball-point pen; double-faced tape; and an assortment of pointed metal styluses and round-edged wooden modeling tools. Found objects such as an orange stick or a demitasse spoon often work well. You will also need: an 11-by-14-inch piece of glass or tempered hardboard; a soft work surface such as a pile of newspapers; spackling compound or plaster of paris; acrylic paint or felt to finish the inside of the box; ½-inch-wide brush; and contact cement prepared for use on non-porous surfaces.

Enlarging the Pattern

To begin, enlarge the design you choose (Figure A or B, opposite) onto a sheet of tracing paper. These patterns are scaled to cover a box top 4 inches square, but you can use either pattern on almost any small box, whatever its shape. The frog design is easy to center, but there may be uneven spaces around the centered fabric design. To fill in these spaces, you can repeat any part of the design. If you add a circle to one corner, however, be sure to repeat it in the remaining three corners for symmetry. Adjust the patterns for the sides of the box top by extending them or widening them until they fit. If you prefer, design your own motifs for the sides by combining simple cross hatching or zigzag bands to complement the main design on the top.

Embossing the Pattern

Place the metal sheet on the soft work surface, face down. Center the pattern tracing, and tape it on the metal. With a light touch, use a blunt tool such as an orange stick or an empty ball-point pen to impress the design lines, fold lines, and cutting lines of the pattern (photograph 1). After all of the lines have been transferred, remove the tracing. Place the metal, face up, on the hard work surface. Just inside the lines just scribed, smooth the metal with a pointed tool (photograph 2). Once the design is clearly defined, turn the metal over again, placing it on the soft work surface. Use a rounded tool, such as a demitasse spoon or a wooden bead, to make dome shapes. If you are embossing the frog design, use a wooden modeling tool (photograph 3) to raise the eyes, limbs, and backbone. Raise all areas slightly to the same low relief. To chase around the raised areas, turn the metal over, put it on the hard work surface, and use a flat-edged tool, such as a popsicle stick, to redefine the edges of the raised areas and to smooth any distortion resulting from stretching the metal from the back (photograph 4). Then use sharp scissors to cut out the pattern, following the cutting lines indicated. When all unpatterned areas are uniformly smooth, work the back of the metal once more on the soft surface, raising the rounded areas until they are as high as you desire. Then impress the final details such as the straight lines inside the circles of the fabric design or the crosshatching on the frog's back. Work gently on these lines to keep from tearing through the thin raised area of the metal.

The design covering the sides of the box top does not have to be as high in relief as that on the top itself. Even a slight embossed pattern here enhances the overall look of the design.

When you have finished embossing your design, thin the spackling compound or plaster of paris with water, following package directions, and brush the mixture into the raised areas, working on the back of the design (photograph 5). This mixture will harden and support the raised areas permanently. Be careful not to let the mixture run onto the smooth surfaces around the filled hollows. Let the mixture dry thoroughly before continuing.

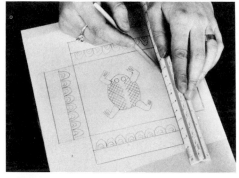

1: Center and tape the enlarged drawing of the box-top pattern (Figure B) on a thin sheet of metal. Transfer the design with a pointed tool like an orange stick, pressing lightly. Use a ruler as a guide when you impress straight lines.

2: With the design transferred, remove the tracing, turn the metal over, and put it on a hard surface for chasing. Press beside the raised lines of the design using a pointed tool to define details more sharply.

You can make a cardboard gift box look like it is worth holding something valuable by covering it with sheet metal. Rich designs can be embossed. Figure A, right, was adapted from a fabric design.

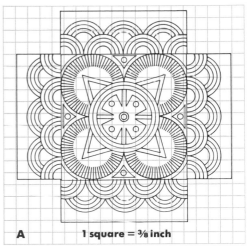

A 1 square = ⅜ inch

Figure A: To enlarge this design, pictured at left, divide a sheet of tracing paper into ⅜-inch squares and copy the pattern square by square. Then, on another sheet of tracing paper, use a pencil and ruler to draw your box top actual size as though it were opened flat. Add an extra ⅜ inch to each edge. Center and tape the enlarged pattern onto the box-top drawing. If you are using a box larger than 4 inches square, you can add designs of your own creation to fill any extra spaces at the edges that seem to need decoration.

3: To raise lines of the design higher, turn the metal face down and lay it on a soft work surface. Use a tool with a rounded tip, like this wooden modeling tool, to push out the relief lines a bit more. This is the repoussé technique.

4: Emboss the design gradually, alternating sides, until the relief is as high as you wish. Then use a tool with a straight edge, such as a popsicle stick, to smooth any distortions in the metal around the design.

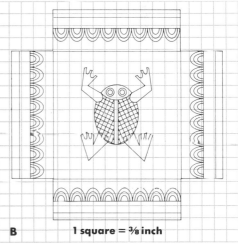

B 1 square = ⅜ inch

Figure B: This alternate design, showing a stylized frog, originated in the Bushango tribe of Congolese Kinshasa. Enlarge the frog on a sheet of tracing paper as directed in Figure A, above, using ⅜-inch squares. Then center and tape this drawing under a drawing of your box top, and you are ready to impress the design on metal.

5: Brush a mixture of spackle or plaster of paris and water into the raised areas. This filling compound will harden to support the shapes. Avoid getting any of the mixture onto unembossed surfaces.

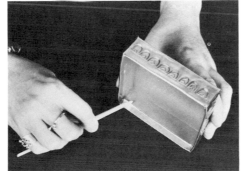

6: Score the sides of the box top with a straight edge so you can fold them downward. Put contact cement on the cardboard box top to hold the metal covering. For a finished edge, press the raw edges inside the lid.

Before gluing any metal to the cardboard box, I paint the inside of the box and lid, and the bottom of the box with acrylic paint, or line the inside with glued-on felt, velvet, or any fabric soft to the touch. If you use fabric, leave the edges free so the metal covering can be folded in under the fabric.

When the paint or glue is dry, cover the sides of the box top with an unembossed strip of metal, as long as the perimeter of the box top and as wide as its side. Beginning in the middle of one side, wrap the strip around the box top. Then remove the strip and score it along the corner folds with a ruler and pencil so you will get a square corner. Apply contact cement to the box-top sides, and glue this strip in place.

Put each side of the metal box-top cover on a soft surface, and score the fold lines with a pencil. Then bend the sides downward from the raised design. Glue the metal cover to the cardboard box top using contact cement. Use the edge of a popsicle stick to flatten the areas around the raised design to insure good contact as the glue sets. Fold the sides of the top in place onto the smooth metal band. Let the glue dry thoroughly before tucking and gluing the projecting raw edges inside the box top for a neat finish (photograph 6, page 1747).

Cover the sides of the bottom part of the box as you covered the sides of the box top, this time adding ½ inch to the width of the strip. Line up one edge of the strip with the bottom edge of the box. Starting in the middle of one side, wrap the metal taut around the perimeter of the box; trim so there is no overlap or gap. Remove the strip and sharply define the bends at the corners with a ruler and pencil, scoring inside the bends. Glue the metal strip to the box using contact cement, rubbing the strip down with a popsicle stick for a neat fit and bond. Let the glue dry before folding the raw edges inside the container.

Jewelry, Lapidary, and Metalwork
Framed in high relief

The hearts-and-flowers mirror frame design in aluminum foil, shown opposite, was inspired by Pennsylvania folk art. At far right, opposite, is an art nouveau motif that has been embossed on copper foil to make a frame for a color drawing, using the same technique. In both cases the thin foil is supported by mat board.

To make a 2¾-inch-wide frame around an 8-by-10-inch mirror, such as the one shown, you will need a 12-by-15-inch piece of 32-gauge aluminum or copper foil; both are available in rolls or sheets at metalcraft and hardware stores. There are many thicknesses of sheet metal, but 32-gauge foil is readily available and easily worked, and aluminum comes in a variety of brilliant colors. In addition to the foil you will need: one 12-by-15-inch sheet of tracing paper; pencil; ruler; 18-by-24-inch hard and soft work surfaces; heavy-duty fabric shears; kitchen scissors; plaster of paris or spackling compound; paintbrush; flat-nosed pliers; steel wool; white glue; contact cement; and an 11-by-14-inch piece of mat board. Do not limit yourself to specialized tools designed for repoussé and chasing work, such as wooden modeling tools and metal styluses. (A pattern tracing wheel, empty ball-point pens, wooden beads and silverware were all used to emboss the mirror frame pictured.) To back and hang the mirror, you will need: a roll of heavy cloth tape; a 2-by-10-inch strip of cardboard; two 11-by-14-inch sheets of cardboard; an 11-by-14-inch piece of colored paper; white glue; an awl or paper punch; and a 12-inch piece of picture wire.

Transferring the Design
The 11-by-14-inch frame, pictured, overlaps the 8-by-10-inch mirror by ¾ inch top and bottom and by 1¼ inches on either side; so the visible mirror measures 5½ by 8½ inches and the metal frame is 2¾ inches wide all around.

To begin the mirror frame, cut a 12-by-15-inch piece of aluminum or copper foil. On a sheet of tracing paper 12 by 15 inches, enlarge the hearts and flowers design (Figure C). Center and tape the tracing on the back of the metal. Use a dull pencil point or a ball-point pen to transfer the outline of each heart and flower, as well as two lines at the inner border and the four dotted lines at the outer edge. Use a light touch. Once the entire design is scribed onto the metal, remove the tracing.

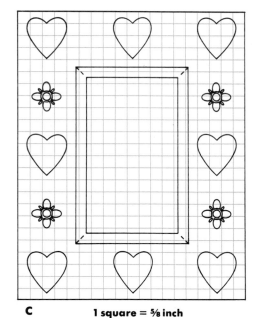

C　　　**1 square = ⅝ inch**

Figure C: To enlarge this design for the mirror frame onto a 12-by-15-inch sheet of tracing paper, first rule the paper into ⅝-inch squares. Then, square by square, copy all of the hearts, flowers, lines, and dashed cutting lines shown.

Folk-art motifs, such as the hearts and flowers often found in the painted designs of the Pennsylvania Dutch, can be embossed on a sheet of metal foil. Here such motifs create a glistening mirror frame made of aluminum.

Metal foil frames can also be used for photographs and drawings such as this art nouveau design.

Hearts and Flowers

Place the metal sheet face down on the soft work surface to begin the first round of repoussé work. This soft cushion will yield just enough to let you depress the metal as you apply pressure to it, and the padding will help protect the front of the metal from getting scratched. To do repoussé work on thin metals, I sometimes abandon all specialized metalworking tools and use found objects instead. Here, I used a miniature toy bowling pin to form the flowers, applying pressure at the very center of each flower and working outward with a gentle circular motion until I reached the edges. Then I used a 1-inch wooden bead to round out the heart shapes (photograph 7). Be sure to apply pressure gradually. It is always possible to apply more pressure to define an area further, but it is almost impossible to correct too deep a stroke. When all the dome-shaped patterns are raised evenly about ⅛ inch, turn the sheet over and put it on the hard work surface. Then chase the front of the metal, using such tools as a metal stylus or a ball-point pen to define the pattern edges of each raised flower and heart (photograph 8). Smooth the metal between

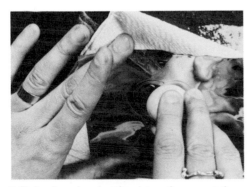

7: To begin embossing the picture frame, put the metal sheet face down on a soft surface such as a thick folded newspaper. Use a rounded tool (here a wooden bead) to raise the dome-shaped hearts and flowers of the design.

8: To define and sharpen the raised designs and eliminate distortion, turn the metal over, move it to a hard surface, and use a pointed tool to smooth around each raised shape. With a popsicle stick flatten the border around each design.

9: Working on the front of the frame, roll a pattern tracing wheel around each heart shape and along the borders of the frame. With this technique, you can impress details of a design in a matter of seconds.

10: To give an antique finish to a frame (here the art noveau picture frame shown on page 1749, brush acrylic paint into all of the crevices of the embossed design. Then use a rag to wipe away most of the paint.

11: Use a craft knife to cut openings in the embossed metal frame and a mat board. The frame opening is smaller, so cuts at each corner let you fold the raw metal edges to the inside of the mat board, concealing the edges of the mat.

12: Glue a mirror to a sheet of cardboard, add picture wire, then place this mat face down on the back of the metal frame. The picture wire should parallel the top of the metal frame. The cardboard will be held to the mat board by the edges of foil that will be folded to the back.

the raised areas using a flat wooden tool such as a popsicle stick or the bowl of a spoon, working slowly in long, even strokes. Make the areas adjacent to the designs as smooth and even as the undecorated border. Some distortion will occur with such thin metal, but careful chasing will minimize it. Turn the piece over again and move it to the soft work surface. Since the flowers are to be lower in relief than the hearts, work only on the heart shapes this time. Raise them evenly to a height of about ⅜ inch; then chase the edges as before. Use a pattern tracing wheel (photograph 9, page 1749) to impress tiny dots around each raised heart and along the inner and outer edges of the frame, working this time on the front of the metal placed on the hard work surface. To support the domed areas, turn the metal over and fill the depressions with plaster of paris or spackling compound. When the mixture hardens, chase the edges of the raised designs. You may want to emboss the raised patterns themselves to add more texture. If you do, be careful to apply only the slightest pressure to the thin metal, and use blunt tools to minimize the danger of making a hole. If you should pierce the metal, you can fill the hole with liquid metal compound (sold in most hardware stores).

Finishing

At this point, the mirror frame is ready to be mounted. But if you want a special finish of some sort, this is the time to apply it. You might like to give the metal a patina, simulating age and the corrosion produced by oxidation. I added a patina to the art nouveau copper picture frame shown on page 1749 by brushing purple acrylic paint over the design, filling all the nooks and crannies, then using a rag to wipe off most of the paint (photograph 10). Patinas can also be simulated with black varnish, india ink, or a small chunk of sulphur diluted with warm water. A Florentine finish can be achieved by rubbing fine steel wool on all the flat surfaces of the design, dulling them while the raised design remains shiny. Copper foil changes color to deeper hues when it is passed over a gas flame. If you try this, avoid burns by handling the foil with copper tongs designed especially for this purpose; then place the hot metal on an asbestos pad to cool.

Cutting the Metal Opening

Use a pencil to deepen the lines at the inner and outer edges, and the fold lines of the frame. Then center the 11-by-14-inch mat beneath the metal, and use a craft knife to cut out a 4½-by-7½-inch metal piece from the center of the frame. This will allow you to turn ½ inch of metal into the opening all around so no raw edges show. Cut a 5½-by-8½-inch opening from the center of the 11-by-14-inch mat board. (Use the craft knife again. Cuts will be 2¾ inches in from the edge on all sides.) Center the mat board on the back of the metal and tape it along its outer edge to the metal. Turn the frame over and use a craft knife to slit the four corners of the metal opening from the front, as indicated by dashed lines in the pattern. This permits you to fold the raw edges of the metal to the inside over the mat board edges (photograph 11). No gluing is needed.

Backing the Frame

Put white glue on one side of an 11-by-14-inch cardboard, and glue a sheet of colored paper to it, to make a finished back for the mirror. When the glue sets, use an awl, nail, or paper punch to make two tiny holes 1½ inches below the top edge, spaced 5 inches apart. Thread the ends of a 12-inch picture wire through each hole. Twist the ends together several times. Put contact cement on the back of the mirror and center it on the uncovered side of the cardboard. Let the glue dry thoroughly. To hold the mirror in place, glue a 2-by-10-inch cardboard strip centered along the bottom edge of the mirror, and run an 8-inch strip of heavy cloth tape along the top edge, overlapping the mirror by no more than ¼ inch so it will not show. Center the mirrored cardboard, face down, on the back of the metal frame so the picture wire is at the top of the frame (photograph 12). To finish, fold the raw edges of the metal frame smoothly over the cardboard back. Use the edge of a knife to press them flat. No glue is needed. Position the shiny mirror frame on a wall where it will reflect a colorful decoration in your room. Or hang it with an arrangement of paintings as a true work of art.

Jewelry, Lapidary, and Metalwork
Necklace of precious leaves

Embossing thick metal requires special steel chisels and hammers, and an evenly resilient surface to support the metal as it is being worked. Softened pitch is an ideal surface for this work, since it offers just the right combination of give and resistance, and it holds the piece in one place. This type of work surface was used for making the silver, bronze, and copper necklace shown below and is generally used for jewelry work.

Prepared burgundy pitch, a compound of ingredients made especially for repoussé work, is available in chunks, but I recommend using pitch that comes pre-melted in heavy metal bowls. The raw chunks have to be melted down; they are flammable and easily ruined by over-cooking. The prepared pitch bowls, however, only need to have the surface softened with a photoflood lamp; supporting rings are available that let you angle the bowl into the most convenient position.

To make a piece of embossed jewelry, you will need 20- or 24-gauge bronze, copper, nickel, sterling silver, or any combination of these. You will also need: a work table; a bench pin (simply a rectangle of wood notched at one end with a V shape to support the metal as it is being sawed); a clamp to hold the bench pin to the table;

Marci Zelmanoff teaches jewelry making at the New School in New York. When she was a teaching assistant at Southern Illinois University, she became interested in wire working and macrame. Her freeform jewelry has been exhibited at New York's Museum of Contemporary Crafts and at many galleries.

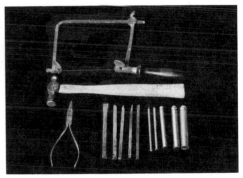

13: Some of the tools you will need to emboss 20- or 24-gauge metal include: a jeweler's saw with No. 4/0 blades (top); a ball peen hammer (center), and from left to right, long-nosed pliers, an assortment of tapered steel chasing and repousse chisels, and round-edged dapping punches.

To make this necklace, the artist cut 12 free-form shapes and a neckband from 24-gauge sheets of silver, copper, and bronze. Each piece of the design was edged with silver solder, and was embossed from the back with dapping punches. Finally, each sculpted form was soldered individually to the neckband.

14: Use a felt-tipped marker or scribe to draw a design on a metal sheet. Place this design over the V opening in a bench pin clamped to the edge of the work table. Then use a jeweler's saw to cut the shape out of the metal sheet.

15: To soften burgundy pitch in a metal pot, direct a photoflood bulb in a reflector lamp onto the surface of the pitch. Once the pitch begins to smell, turn off the light and let the pitch cool slightly.

jeweler's shears; wire cutters; permanent felt-tipped marker or tracing scribe; pad of tracing paper; pencil; rubber cement; rubber-cement pickup; jeweler's saw; No. 4/0 jeweler's saw blades; small half-round file; flat file; and the prepared burgundy pitch. In addition you will need: 11-by-14-inch asbestos pad; No. 1 photoflood bulb and clip-on lamp with a reflector shade; small- and medium-sized ball peen hammers; assortment of round-ended dapping punches; flat- and sharp-edged chisels; fuel-in-hand propane-gas torch; dry pickle mix; wide-mouthed glass jar; rubber gloves; 10-inch forceps; copper tongs; felt buffing rod; tripoli and rouge polishing compounds; and long-nosed pliers. Some specialized tools are shown in photograph 13, page 1751.

If you plan to solder jewelry pieces together, as I did with the piece pictured, you will also need: 500-grit emery paper or 4/0 steel wool; fine-tipped paintbrush; liquid soldering flux; small porcelain dish; some so-called easy silver solder; and an iron scribe to manipulate the molten solder. There are other ways to assemble jewelry, of course. If you prefer not to solder, you could drill holes in the individual parts and join them with rings, available from jewelry supply companies. Or you could simply make a single repoussé pendant to suspend from a chain or metal choker.

Practice Pieces
A good deal of work goes into making jewelry, even if the piece is simple. You will need to master the techniques of sawing precise shapes out of metal, doing the repoussé work and chasing, finishing each worked piece, and in some cases, joining the parts into one piece of jewelry. Before you attempt a complex piece, practice on some very simple things, as follows. To start, use a sharp-pointed scribe or a felt-tipped marker to outline a design directly on a piece of metal. Clamp the bench pin to the work table so the V-shaped end projects. Put a No. 4/0 blade in the jeweler's saw, with the teeth pointed downward, so any raggedness from the cut will be on the bottom of the piece of metal. Holding the metal over the V opening, saw with steady up-and-down strokes—any forcing will snap the delicate blade. Cut the metal along the line drawn (photograph 14). If you need to cut out a piece from the center, drill a small hole at any point inside the cutting line, thread the saw blade through the hole, clamp the blade in the saw frame, and cut.

Once the metal has been cut to shape, draw the repoussé design on the back and prepare the pitch to support it. Simply soften the surface of the pitch in the pitch bowl by positioning the clip-on lamp so the photoflood bulb shines on the pitch surface (photograph 15). As soon as the pitch begins to smell, remove the lamp. If the pitch gets too hot it will lose its holding ability, and if it gets too soft, it will cover the edges of the metal, making them hard to work. Let the pitch cool until the surface is barely sticky; then put the metal piece on it.

To emboss the design, hold a chisel or a dapping punch at a slight angle to the back of the metal, and tap it lightly with a small ball peen hammer, as you follow the lines of the design (photograph 16). It takes a lot of practice to get consistently good results. I used round-ended dapping punches to give a bumpy texture to each piece of the necklace pictured, but I suggest that you experiment with tools of many different shapes to see what effect each contributes to a design. And while you are experimenting, try applying varying amounts of pressure to a tool to see how deep a design you can make without punching through the metal. If a piece of metal begins to sink too far into the pitch, move it to another spot. If the metal is not easily removed, reheat the surface of the pitch.

The process of making a repoussé design in metal with punches usually hardens the metal, and it may become too brittle to work. If that happens, you will need to anneal the metal in order to finish the design. To do this, put the metal on an asbestos pad and heat it with the propane torch until the metal turns dull red. Then let the metal cool. Annealing metal softens it, but it also deposits oxides on the surface. To remove these, an acid bath, followed by a rinse in cold water, will suffice. To prepare the acid bath, fill a wide-mouthed gallon jug with water. Add the dry pickle mix, following package directions and wearing rubber gloves in case you are sensitive to the chemicals. Using copper tongs to avoid contaminating the metal, lower it into the solution and leave it five minutes. Then use the tongs to remove the metal, and hold it under cold running water for one minute. Reheat the pitch before you attempt additional work on the metal.

When the repoussé work is done, lift the metal off the pitch. If the surface of the pitch is pockmarked, reheat it with the lamp until the work surface is smooth again. Now you are ready to chase the front side of the metal piece, defining and accenting the raised pattern by smoothing the areas between. To use a chasing tool, hold it vertically and keep it constantly in contact with the metal, as you slide it around and give it light taps with a ball peen hammer. When you have finished chasing, remove the metal from the pitch, melt away any pitch that sticks to it using a propane torch, and give it a final rinse in the pickle bath and cold water.

Making Jewelry

The necklace I designed, shown on page 1751, is made of 12 free-form shapes, each 1 to 2 inches wide and 4 to 9 inches long. These were soldered to a metal strip about 1½ by 10 inches that serves as a neck ring. In planning a design of your own, take into account how you will assemble the pieces. Even if you plan only a simple pendant, you will need to plan for the hole that will hold the ring that will attach the pendant to a chain. If you plan to outline pieces with solder, then fuse them together, keep the shapes simple, and make sure they will fit together comfortably when the jewelry is being worn.

Use tracing paper to draw a full-sized pattern for the piece of jewelry you want to make; then with rubber cement stick the patterns to the metal. If one edge of a pattern lines up with an edge of metal, you will minimize waste.

Use the jeweler's saw to cut out the metal pieces. To finish the raw edge of the cut piece of metal, smooth it with a small file. Apply pressure only on the forward stroke of the file; lift the file on the back stroke so you do not dull its teeth. When all edges are smooth to the touch, remove the tracing and rubber cement.

Before embossing the metal pieces, prepare them for assembly either by running a line of silver solder around the edge of each piece or by drilling holes to accommodate jump rings. If you use solder, clean the edge of each piece with emery paper or fine steel wool to remove any grease or oil that might hinder fusion. Then place the clean metal on an asbestos pad. Brush liquid flux onto the edges of the metal wherever you want solder to adhere. Flux prevents the formation of oxides and facilitates the flow of solder. Fit a loop of solder around each metal shape. Wearing double-cotton work gloves and goggles for protection, light the propane torch, following the manufacturer's directions. Adjust the flame until there is a bright 2-inch blue cone. Hold the torch over the metal so the tip of the blue cone touches the solder. Use a slow, circular motion so the solder will melt uniformly onto the edge of the piece (photograph 17). Lower the solder-edged piece of metal into the pickling solution using copper tongs; then rinse the piece with cold water, and dry it before placing it on the pitch for embossing.

To emboss the metal pieces, use the same techniques you used on the practice pieces. Once all of the pieces are embossed, polish the finished shapes with a felt buffing rod, first applying tripoli compound to the metal with a rag. This mild abrasive will remove surface scratches. Finally, wipe rouge compound over the surface and give it a final polishing to bring out its lustre.

Assembling Jewelry

Once all the pieces have been embossed and polished, you are ready to assemble the piece of jewelry. If you use rings, simply open the rings with long-nosed pliers, insert them in their holes, and close the rings. If you use solder and want to join the pieces to each other or to a neck band, you will have to direct the propane gas flame precisely at each spot being joined; or else the joints already soldered might melt.

When I made the necklace pictured, I joined each individual piece directly to a preshaped neck band. To do this, I had allowed an extra inch of solder at the top of each piece when I originally edged it with solder. Before joining the pieces to the neck band, I embossed the neck band itself and curved it into the circular shape. Finally, keeping the extra solder strands on top, I arranged the polished free-form pieces until I was satisfied with the design. By directing the flame carefully at the precise joint being fused, I was able to attach one piece at a time to the neck ring. The silver solder itself is decorative; heated, it makes bright, tiny beads.

For related entries, see "American Indian Crafts," "Jewelry," "Silversmithing," and "Tin and Pierced Work."

16: Lay the flat metal shape on the surface of the tacky pitch. Use a ball peen hammer to tap the end of a dapping punch or tapered chisel to do the repoussé work of the design. Lift the metal off the pitch and turn it over for chasing.

17: To create a necklace of the type shown on page 1751, wrap individual pieces with solder before you emboss them. To do this, fit a loop of solder around the edge of each piece, leaving a 1-inch piece of solder wire free at one end. With a propane gas torch, melt the band of solder onto the metal edge.

REVERSE APPLIQUÉ
Spectacular Cutaways

Reverse appliqué differs from traditional appliqué in that rather than adding small pieces of fabric on top of a larger background fabric to form a design, you begin by basting together a sandwich of several layers of fabrics of different colors. Then you form the design by slitting or cutting away selected areas of the top layers of fabric, exposing different colors in the desired shapes. The cut edges are turned under and sewn by hand using tiny stitches. While this technique is somewhat more complicated than traditional appliqué, reverse appliqué is really quite simple to do. The extra planning and imagination it requires make it more challenging, and therefore a more exciting needlecraft.

Reverse appliqué is a technique favored by Loretta Holz, a crafts writer and designer. She is the author of Teach Yourself Stitchery, *a book for children;* Mobiles You Can Make; *and* Many Ways to Sell What You Make: A Marketing Guide for Artists and Craftspeople. *She has designed for many magazines, including* Creative Crafts, McCall's Needlework and Crafts, Woman's Day, Lady's Circle, *and* Golden Hands Monthly.

Cuna Indian women wear *mola* blouses, and not just for special occasions. Some have more than two dozen, each representing hours of hand-stitching on two to seven layers of colorful cotton cloth.

Molas

Reverse appliqué plays an important part in the culture of the Cuna Indians, who live on the San Blas islands off the coast of Panama. According to Cuna tradition, there is a special place in heaven reserved for artists, and the women of this proud, independent society are world famous for their striking reverse appliqué panels, called *molas* (opposite).

The Cunas have no written language, so there is no record of the development of the *mola*. However, it is assumed that the influence of nineteenth-century missionaries and the new availability of brightly colored cotton fabrics brought by traders were a combination volatile enough to cause the women, who used to paint their bodies, to give up their paint and paintbrushes in favor of needles, thread, and cloth. The word *mola* originally meant clothing but has come to mean a woman's blouse, with a front and back decorated with panels of reverse appliqué (above). In response to tourist demand, the Cunas now produce the panels separately. Such *mola* panels (one is featured here as a project) can be incorporated into utilitarian objects—lampshades, pillows, cushions, skirts, jackets, dresses, or tote bags—as well as blouses. Or they can simply be appreciated for their own beauty and hung on the wall as works of art.

Cuna Indians of the San Blas islands produce the world's most spectacular reverse-appliqué panels, which they call *molas*. The *mola* opposite is a fine example of the Cunas' remarkable talent for transforming any scene or object—in this case, flowers—into a dramatic and stylized pattern. The balanced design, sophisticated colors, and meticulous workmanship (note the hand-stitched rickrack) are qualities that the best *mola* makers strive to incorporate in their work.

Materials

Most of the materials required for reverse appliqué are those used for any sewing project: fabric; thread; needles; scissors; straight pins; and tailor's chalk. Lightweight cotton fabric is traditionally used for reverse appliqué and is the best for this type of work. You may use any crisp, tightly woven, lightweight fabric (such as a cotton-and-polyester blend), but pure polyester is a poor choice. The coarser the weave, the more difficult it becomes to keep the turned-under edges from popping out and raveling. The thread you use should match the color of each fabric layer except the bottom one. In addition, you will need: paper, ruler, and pencil (to make the patterns); and a pair of small, sharp-pointed scissors such as embroidery scissors.

1: To start a reverse appliqué, baste the layers of fabric together all around the edges. This practice swatch consists of three layers.

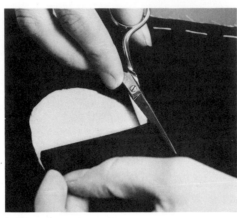

2: To cut out a shape, first pierce the top layer of fabric with the scissors. Then make short, controlled snips to avoid cutting the underlayer.

3: Turn under and sew all around the edge, making tiny stitches that are perpendicular to the edge on the right side but diagonal underneath.

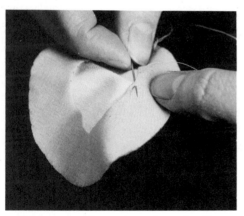

4: The procedure for turning under and sewing the cut edge of lower layers is the same as for sewing the top layer.

Procedure

The technique, once mastered, is a simple one, but you should practice cutting and stitching an experimental swatch before you begin any project. Cut three pieces of pressed fabric, each approximately 7 inches square. Place the squares together, raw edges even. Baste through all three layers to keep them from shifting as you cut and stitch (photograph 1). In the center of the swatch, pick up the top layer of fabric. Pierce the fabric with the sharp points of the scissors; cut out a shape and remove it (photograph 2). When you work from a pattern, cut ⅛ inch inside the marked outline to provide a turn-under allowance. Thread a needle with thread that matches the top layer of fabric; knot the end. With the point of the needle, poke the cut edge under ⅛ inch; hold it down with the thumb of your free hand. To begin sewing, bring the needle up from the back to the front through all layers of fabric, catching a few threads of the turned-under edge. Then insert the needle from front to back through the under layers, making a tiny stitch that is perpendicular to the fold. Bring the needle up diagonally through all three layers, again catching the folded edge (photograph 3). Continue stitching in this fashion until the entire cut edge of the top layer has been folded under and stitched down. To end a thread, take a few small stitches through the bottom layer where they will not show. To cut shapes from subsequent layers, follow the same procedure, again choosing thread that matches the layer being sewn down (photograph 4).

Helpful Hints

When you fold and stitch tight curves, you will find it easier to fold the edge under if you make tiny clips in the turn-under allowance. You may find that you prefer to turn under the entire edge of a cut-out section and secure it with pins before you begin to stitch, rather than turning it under bit by bit as you sew. When you work with larger pieces of fabric, add lines of basting stitches diagonally across the layers to keep them from shifting. You can easily snip away these large stitches if they get in your way while you work. Since keeping the fabric flat and unpuckered is important, press the fabric before you begin, and again each time you complete a step. Sewing around tiny cut-out circles is the most difficult of all reverse appliqué steps. If the design calls for small circles, cut them out of a scrap of fabric and appliqué them on top, turning the edge under and using the same stitching technique.

Designing Your Own

There are many sources of reverse appliqué designs. The photographs below will give you some ideas, but keep your eyes open for others. Fabrics, flowers, book jackets, and designs worked in other techniques such as embroidery, mosaics, stained glass, and patchwork suggest patterns that can be adapted for reverse appliqué.

A quick way to try out a design is to experiment with construction paper. Arrange layers of paper that correspond to the colors of the fabrics you intend to use. Staple the layers together at one side; then cut the planned design one layer at a time, holding the other layers aside as you cut.

Some Cuna Indians draw a design on the fabric, but most work without a pattern. They plunge right in, and cut and stitch with an assurance born of years of experience. You may eventually do the same, but at the beginning cut a paper pattern for each section of your design. Pin the pattern in place on the fabric, and trace around the edge with tailor's chalk. Then cut the fabric ⅛ inch inside the chalk line, and turn the fabric under along the line.

When you baste the fabric layers together, place the color that you want to appear most often directly below the top layer. This way you avoid cutting through more than one layer unnecessarily. Occasionally you may want to go directly to the third or fourth layer, bypassing intermediate layers so they do not show at all. To do this, cut the design from the top layer as usual. Then reach through the opening, and cut away the second layer (and the third and fourth if necessary) until you reveal the desired layer. Cut the intermediate layers farther back than the top opening; then stitch the top layer to the layer you want to show.

Experiment with small-patterned fabrics as well as solid colors. Heavy fabric is hard to turn under neatly, but you might use one for the bottom layer, which is not cut. And try using felt—the cut edges need not be turned under since they do not ravel, so they can be glued down instead of sewn.

The Cuna Indians believe that bathing the hands of a woman in a potion made from the leaves of a special tree will inspire her to create wonderful *mola* designs. These details were all taken from authentic Cuna *molas;* they might serve as your inspiration when you design your own.

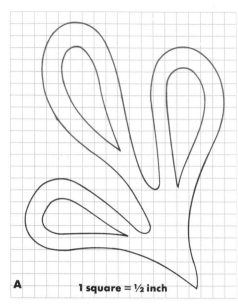

A **1 square = ½ inch**

Figure A: To make a quarter-pattern for the splash design, copy this pattern onto paper that you have ruled in ½-inch squares. Transfer the lines, one square at a time, onto the larger grid.

Needlecrafts
Splashes

Although there are six colors in the reverse appliqué design of the pillow top pictured below, only three layers of fabric were used. The multihued middle layer is made by sewing four pieces of fabric together, patchwork fashion.

Materials
For the top and bottom layers of the pillow top, and for the back of the pillow, you will need: three 22-by-26-inch pieces of fabric (two black and one red); for the middle layer you will need: four 13½-by-11½-inch pieces of fabric (pink, green, yellow, and blue). You will also need: thread to match each fabric except the bottom layer; an 11-by-13-inch piece of paper for the pattern; ruler; pencil; tailor's chalk; straight pins; sewing needle; iron and ironing board; small and large scissors. The pillow form requires two 22-by-26-inch pieces of muslin or other inexpensive, lightweight fabric, and polyester fiber filling for stuffing.

Making the Pillow
To begin, enlarge the quarter-pattern (Figure A), and cut along the outer edge of the splash. Put aside the pattern. Stitch the four small fabric rectangles together to form one larger piece. To do this, place two rectangles together, right sides facing; sew along one shorter side, making a ½-inch seam and forming a strip. Press the seam to one side. Sew the two remaining rectangles together the same way. Then sew the two strips together, forming a 22-by-26-inch rectangle, and press the seam to one side. Place this middle layer between the black layer and the red layer (Figure B). Baste the layers together around the edges and diagonally across.

With tailor's chalk, divide the pillow top into quarter sections. Pin the pattern to it, centering the pattern within one of the quarters. Trace around the edge of the pattern with tailor's chalk, and remove the pattern. Referring to the directions and photographs on page 1756, cut the top layer of fabric ⅛ inch inside the chalk line, exposing the patchwork fabric underneath. Using black thread to match the top layer, turn under the cut edge and stitch all around. Cut the top layer a little at a

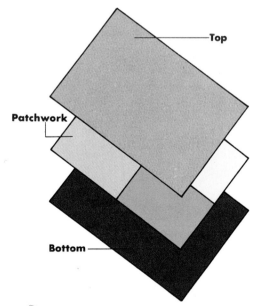

Top
Patchwork
Bottom

B
Figure B: You will need only three layers if you make a four-color patchwork layer for the center of your sandwich, placing it between the black top layer and the red bottom layer.

This pillow, with its large, bold splashes of color, demonstrates how dramatic reverse appliqué can be. But the cutting and sewing are easy enough to make this a good first project in this technique.

time, and make sure your stitches penetrate all three layers. Next, cut out the tear-drop-shaped inner sections of the pattern. Pin these patterns in place on the pillow top, and trace around their edges with tailor's chalk. Cut through the middle fabric layer, exposing the red bottom layer of the fabric. Using thread to match the middle layer, turn under the cut edges and stitch them to the bottom layer. Repeat this procedure for each of the four quarters of the pillow top, revealing each color in turn.

To finish the pillow cover, place the pillow top and the pillow back together, right sides facing. Sew all around, making ½-inch seams. Round the corners as you sew, and leave a 10-inch opening on one short side. Clip the raw edges in to the seam at the rounded corners; then turn the pillow cover right side out. To make the inner pillow, sew the two muslin pieces together as you did the outer pillow. Turn the inner pillow cover right side out and stuff it with polyester fiber filling. Fold the raw edges of the opening ½ inch to the inside; sew the opening closed by hand with tiny stitches. Insert this pillow in the pillow cover; stitch the cover opening closed by hand.

Needlecrafts
Cat tote bag

¢ ◻ ♦ 🍃

This design adds several advanced techniques to the basic procedure of sewing reverse appliqué (page 1756). The narrow stripes on the cat's back are just slits with the edges turned under and stitched down. A small piece of yellow fabric was added only for the face. Finally, embroidery was used to represent the cat's whiskers, a detail that could not be defined successfully in reverse appliqué.

Materials
To make the tote you will need fabric in the following colors and amounts: ½ yard each of solid red (for the outside layer of the tote) and red print (for the lining); one black and one blue piece measuring 12 inches square (for the second and third layers); and one 3-inch square of yellow (for the face). You will also need: red and black sewing thread; a small amount of yellow embroidery thread; paper for the pattern; pencil; ruler; a single-edged razor blade; tailor's chalk; small and large scissors; straight pins; and a needle.

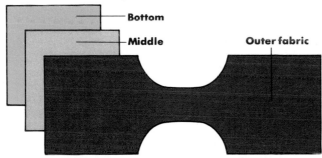

D

Figure D: To assemble the fabrics for cutting, pin and baste the blue bottom layer, the black middle layer, and the top red layer together, keeping bottom (left) and side edges even.

Making the Tote
Enlarge the pattern (Figure C) for the tote and the reverse appliqué design. To cut out the tote, place the outer fabric and the lining fabric together; fold in half cross-wise, forming four layers. Pin the pattern to the four layers with the top of the pattern on the folded edge of the fabric. Cut out the outer tote and lining, following the outer line of the pattern. Set aside the lining.

Pin the blue bottom layer, the black middle layer, and the red top layer together (Figure D). Baste around the edges. Cut out the cat design from the pattern, using the razor blade to slit the stripes on the cat's back, and eyes, nose, and mouth. Pin the cat pattern to the tote in the position shown in Figure C. With tailor's chalk, trace around the pattern; unpin the pattern. Following the photographs and directions on page 1756, cut the cat shape from the red fabric only, revealing the black fabric underneath. Cut ⅛ inch inside the marked outline, a little at a time, and use

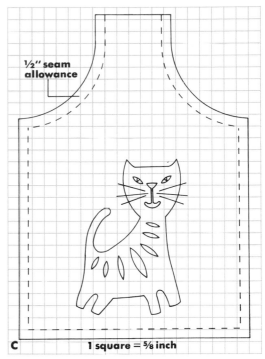

C   1 square = ⅝ inch

Figure C: Enlarge this pattern for a tote bag by copying it onto paper that you have ruled into ⅝-inch squares. Transfer both the outline of the tote and the cat design to the larger grid, copying the lines one square at a time.

If you are a cat fancier, you will especially appreciate this reverse appliqué tote, a handy size for either women or girls.

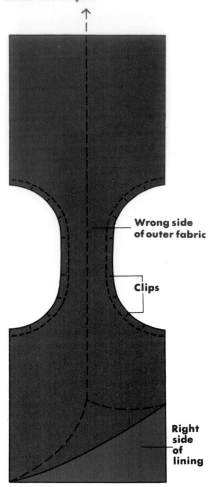

E

Figure E: Stitch the lining and outer fabric pieces together, right sides facing, along the curved edges, making ½-inch seams. Clip into the seam allowance as necessary to ease the curves. Then turn the tote bag right side out by pulling one end through the sewn middle section as indicated by the arrow.

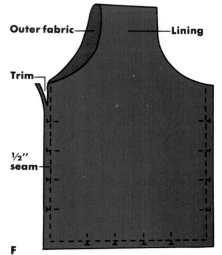

F

Figure F: With the lining facing the outside, pin, then stitch the front and back sections of the tote together from curve to curve. Make a ½-inch seam, and round the corners. Before turning the tote right side out, trim the seam.

red thread to stitch down the folded-under edge. When the cat design has been entirely stitched, pin the cat pattern back on the tote. With tailor's chalk, trace the cut-out shapes on the back and face. Remove the pattern, and slit the black fabric along the center of the marked areas. Clip into the seam allowance around the back slits, and turn the edge under along the chalk lines, exposing the blue fabric underneath. Sew the edges down, forming stripes. Insert the piece of yellow fabric underneath. Sew the edges down, forming stripes. Insert the piece of yellow fabric between the second and third layers by slipping it through the nose-and-mouth slit. Pin or baste it in place. Clip into the seam allowance around small curves, fold the cut edges under along the marked lines, and stitch down with black thread. To finish the cat, make two long stitches with black sewing thread for the pupil of each eye; for the whiskers, make six longer stitches with yellow embroidery thread.

Place the outer tote and the lining together, right sides facing, with edges even. Following Figure E, stitch along the curved edges, making ½-inch seams. Then turn the tote right side out. Press well, especially along the seams. Then pin the front and back sections together with the lining on the outside. Stitch together as shown in Figure F. Trim the seam, and finish with a zigzag stitch or cover the edge with bias tape. Turn the tote right side out and press well.

This *mola* panel with a stylized bird as the motif was worked by a Cuna Indian woman. Such bright effects are achieved by inserting small fabric swatches of various colors between the top and bottom layers and exposing them in limited areas.

Needlecrafts
San Blas bird

The Cuna Indian woman seeks a fresh approach with each *mola* she undertakes. Even though she may use a traditional design, no two *molas* are exactly alike. Native flowers, animals, and birds are often stylized almost into abstractions. But the Cunas have a subtle sense of humor that is often reflected in *molas* that tell a story. Panels may depict a medicine man's incantations gone awry; or lobster and fish brandishing knives and forks in anticipation of a dinner consisting of a man sitting in a casserole. There are even *molas* showing women making *molas*. Although the directions that follow allow you to duplicate the *mola* above, in the true spirit of *mola* making you may prefer to choose and arrange your own color inserts.

Materials

To make the reverse appliqué bird panel in the colors shown, you will need two 15-by-20-inch pieces of fabric, one red (top layer) and one white (bottom layer); 17 small pieces of fabric (about 3 by 4 inches) in assorted colors such as light and dark blue, black, pink, yellow, orange, light and dark green, and brown; red sewing thread; paper for the pattern; pencil; ruler; small and large scissors; straight pins; and a sewing needle. If you wish to use the panel as a hanging, you will also need two 5-inch squares (for the hanging tabs), one 15-by-20-inch piece of red fabric (for the backing), and a 19-inch wooden dowel.

Making the Hanging

With raw edges even, place the top red layer and the bottom white layer of fabric together; baste all around the edges and diagonally from corner to corner. Enlarge the pattern for the bird (Figure G). Cut out the bird shape, including the eye, and pin it, centered, on top of the red fabric. Trace around the pattern edges with tailor's chalk, and remove the pattern. Then draw straight lines to indicate the slits, using a ruler and tailor's chalk (refer to the photograph opposite as a guide).

To do the reverse appliqué, begin with the outline of the bird and the slits in the wings, tail, and feet that radiate from the outline. Working on one small area at a

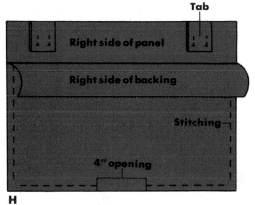

H

Figure H: To turn the panel into a wall hanging, pin the tabs to the right side of the top edge of the panel, raw edges even, 2 inches in from either side. Pin the backing fabric on top, raw edges matching. Stitch together, making ½-inch seams, but leave a 4-inch opening so you can turn the panel right side out. The tabs will be held in the seam.

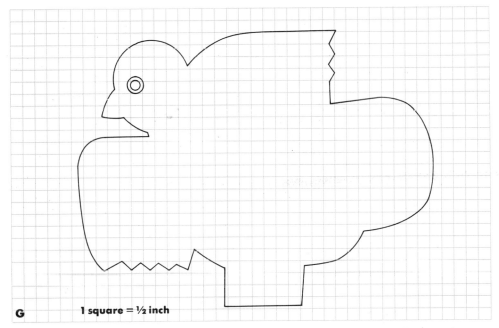

G **1 square = ½ inch**

Figure G: To enlarge this bird pattern, draw a grid whose squares measure ½-inch; then copy the pattern one square at a time.

time, slit along the marked line through the top layer only. Then turn the edges under ⅛ inch, revealing the white fabric underneath, and stitch them down with red thread (see page 1756 for basic directions). Next, cut and stitch the eye, and appliqué a small black circle within it. Make small scattered cuts in the head area; fold edges under and stitch down to form dots. Then cut and stitch the slits that will be white. Finally, cut and stitch the slits that are various colors. For each group, slip a piece of colored fabric through the first slit you cut before you stitch it down. Position each insert so it shows through as in the photograph. Some inserts must be irregularly shaped to fit, such as the brown piece to the left of the beak.

To finish the panel as a hanging, fold each of the two 5-inch squares in half, and stitch them together along the long edge, forming two tubes. Turn each tube right side out, and fold in half, making tabs. Pin the red backing and the finished panel together, right sides facing, with the tabs between (Figure H). Stitch together, leaving an opening so you can turn the panel right side out. Press well, turning the raw edges of the opening in ½ inch. Sew the opening closed by hand using tiny stitches. Insert the dowel in the loops, and hang on the wall.

For related entries, see "Appliqué" and "Embroidery."

RIBBONCRAFT
Rainbow Fabrications

Ribbons have been a part of human decoration ever since fashion became a consideration. Records of such decoration date back to biblical times; in the book of Numbers, Moses directed the Israelites to make garments with borders decorated with blue ribbons. Nor has the use of ribbon been limited to decoration of garments. Egyptian tomb paintings show women wearing narrow ribbons called fillets over their foreheads. Virgil, in the *Aeneid*, describes similar ribbon headbands worn by men and women of ancient Greece.

Ribbon appeared in Europe around the eleventh century; it was then a strip of woven cloth with decoration woven or embroidered onto it. This was cut into lengths which were sewn onto garments.

Ribbon as it is made today, with two selvage (woven) edges, did not appear until the sixteenth century. The most luxurious ribbon of that time had gold or silver thread woven into it, making it very expensive. Ribbon garters, popular with both men and women of fashion, were often made from such ribbons; sometimes they were further ornamented with diamonds and gold lace. The English parliament prohibited tradespeople from wearing ribbons, thus reserving them for the nobility.

By the middle of the seventeenth century, however, people of all classes were again wearing them. Men's clothing was as decorated as women's. One costume made for a man during the English Restoration period (1660-1689), on display at the Victoria and Albert Museum, contains 250 yards of ribbon. Ribbons were worn from head to toe, from shoes trimmed with ribbon rosettes to elaborate headdresses made of wired ribbon. When used in such quantity, ribbons emphasized the wearer's social standing because no one so ornately adorned could possibly do anything. Thus, ribbons became a symbol of the idle rich.

In colonial America, little ribbon was worn, due to a combination of anti-English feeling, the Puritans' severe style of dress, and the cost of imported ribbon. Splendor in dress waned in England and continental Europe as well. But by the beginning of the nineteenth century, ribbons for decoration were coming into vogue again. The first American ribbon factory was opened in Philadelphia in 1815. By the mid-1800s, ornate ribbon creations were back in style, as shown by the bonnets at right. They appeared in *Godey's Magazine and Lady's Book*, a fashion magazine, in 1854.

Ribbon Prizes

From county fairs to military ceremonies, ribbons are awarded to recognize excellence. Traditionally, a blue ribbon symbolizes the highest honor, and a red ribbon, the next. This custom comes from the English. Blue, symbolizing purity, was used to designate the Order of the Garter, the highest order of English knighthood. A red ribbon designated the Order of the Bath, the next highest in rank.

Modern Uses

Today ribbon can be used to decorate everything from clothing to trays to tennis-racket covers, as projects that follow show. Ribbons are fun to work with because they come in myriad colors, designs, and textures. You can combine polka dots with stripes, plaids with prints, velvet with satin, grosgrain with moiré—whatever your imagination suggests. The width of the ribbons you choose will affect the final design. The narrower the ribbon, the more you will need to cover a given area. The wider the ribbon, the more its color and pattern will dominate the design. The fabric content of the ribbon will determine whether the finished project can be washed or must be dry-cleaned. When you decorate washable clothing such as the T shirt on page 1773, use washable ribbon, and preshrink it by washing it in warm water.

Jermaine Sonnenschein discovered the beauty of ribbons when making patchwork pillows with ribbon trim. Intrigued, she experimented with making all-ribbon pillows. The results are shown opposite. Jermaine has made pillows professionally for individuals and interior decorators and has exhibited pillows at the Brooklyn Heights Promenade Art Show and the Washington Square Outdoor Art Show, both in New York.

These ribbon bonnets are the fashion for the coming season, says *Godey's Magazine and Lady's Book*. The season is spring of 1854.

Displayed on her living room couch for all to admire are some of the many different ribbon pillows that Jermaine Sonnenschein has made. They indicate the great variety of designs that can be achieved with ribbons.

Woven ribbon pillow

Ribbons of varying designs and widths, woven together, make a pillow cover of striking design.

Patterned ribbons of varying widths can be woven together to form an unusual pillow cover like the one above. Your choice of ribbons—patterns mixed with solid colors, narrow ¼-inch widths mixed with wide 2-inch widths, subtle prints mixed with bold graphic designs—will make your pillow unique. You can coordinate the colors with a sofa or a bedspread, or choose colors at random and be surprised by the design that emerges, or choose ribbons in a single color family for a monochromatic look.

To make a pillow similar to the one pictured, you will need: ½ yard polyester-and-cotton fabric to back the ribbons; ½ yard taffeta for the back cover of the pillow; ¾ yard of 45-inch-wide fabric, color-coordinated with the ribbons, for the ruffle; thread; a 14-inch-square knife-edge pillow form or loose stuffing of polyester fiber; and ribbons. The amount of ribbon needed will vary depending on the width used, but there are some guidelines to help you estimate the total. Each piece of ribbon in the pillow is approximately ½ yard long. If you plan to use one kind of ribbon for a horizontal and a vertical band, you will need about 1 yard of that ribbon. In all, you will need enough ribbon to cover a 15-by-15-inch square twice. If you choose 1½-or 2-inch-wide ribbons, you will need only eight or nine lengths for each direction. If you use ¼-and ½-inch ribbons, you will need more than 30 lengths. As you choose your ribbons, add the widths together until you reach a total of about 30 inches.

Before starting the pillow, cut all fabric and ribbon to the correct size. Cut a 15-inch square of polyester-and-cotton fabric to back the ribbon and a 15-inch square of taffeta to back the pillow. Cut each ribbon 15¼ inches long. Place the ribbons that will be vertical on the ribbon-backing fabric, and shift them around until you are pleased with the arrangement. (They will look different when they are woven.)

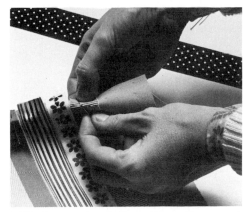

1: The first step in weaving a ribbon pillow cover is to pin the vertical ribbons to the fabric backing, starting ¼ inch from the left side and leaving 1/16 inch between ribbons.

2: Arrange the horizontal ribbons on top of the vertical ribbons, leaving 1/16 inch between ribbons. Pin them to the ¼ inch of backing fabric exposed at the left.

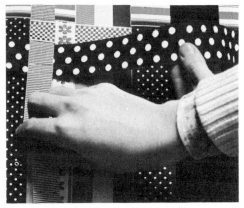

3: After stitching across the top and down the left side, weave the first horizontal ribbon over the first vertical ribbon and under the second, continuing across. Weave the second horizontal ribbon the opposite way: under the first, over the second, and so forth. Continue until all ribbons are woven.

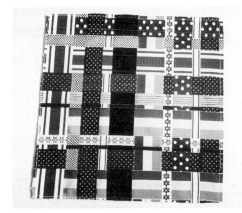

4: When all the ribbons have been woven, pin and stitch the free ribbon ends to the fabric backing, along the right side and across the bottom.

5: Pin the raw edge of the gathered ruffle to the raw edge of the woven-ribbon square, with the ruffle lying on the inside of the square.

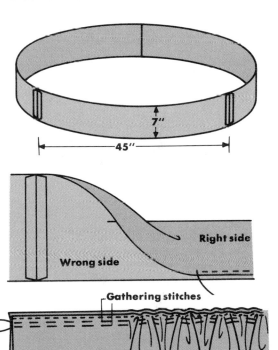

Figure A: To make a ruffle, join three strips of fabric into a loop and press the seams open (top). Fold the circle in half lengthwise with wrong sides facing and press; then stitch ⅛ inch in from the raw edge (center). Make two machine-sewn rows of basting stitches, and pull the top threads to gather the ruffle (bottom).

Starting ¼ inch in from the left side, pin these ribbons in place leaving a 1/16-inch space between them (photograph 1). Pin the top of the ribbon, leaving the bottom free. Place the horizontal ribbons on top of the vertical ones, arranging them to your liking and leaving a 1/16-inch space between them. Pin the left end of each horizontal ribbon to the ¼ inch of backing fabric exposed on the left side (photograph 2). Leave the right ends of the ribbons free. Stitch all the ribbons to the backing fabric a scant ¼ inch from the edge of the fabric, along the top and left sides. Make sure you do not catch the first vertical ribbon when you stitch over the horizontal ribbons and vice versa.

Weaving the Ribbons
To weave the ribbons, flip the horizontal ribbons to the side of the pillow cover, leaving the vertical ribbons covering the fabric (photograph 3). Weave the first horizontal ribbon over the first vertical ribbon, under the second, and so forth to the end. Weave the second horizontal ribbon the opposite way, under the first vertical ribbon, over the second, and so forth. When all ribbons are woven, pin all free ends. Then stitch the free ends down ¼ inch from the edge of the backing fabric (photograph 4).

To make the ruffle, cut three 7-by-45-inch strips of fabric. Join the three pieces into a circle, and press the seams open (Figure A, top). Fold the circle in half lengthwise, with wrong sides facing, and press. Stitch ⅛ inch in from the raw edges (Figure A, center) to make a 3⅜-inch-wide loop. To gather the ruffle, make two rows of large basting stitches with your sewing machine, keeping both rows within ½ inch of the raw edge. Pull on the top threads, easing the fabric along these threads (Figure A, bottom). Gather the fullness along the stitching until the raw

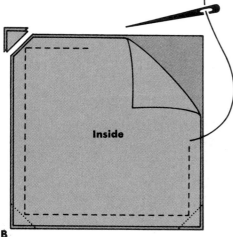

6: With the pillow-backing fabric right side down, place it over the ribbon square and ruffle; then pin all three layers with raw edges matching, and stitch them together (Figure B).

B

Figure B: Sew the pillow front and back together, right sides facing, catching the ruffle in the seam and stitching ½ inch in from the edge. Leave a 10-inch opening along one edge for stuffing, and so you can turn the cover right side out. Trim the corners.

edge measures 60 inches, the outside measurement of the pillow cover. Pin the raw edge of the ruffle to the raw edge of the woven-ribbon square (photograph 5, page 1765). Be sure the ruffle makes a sharp turn as it goes around each corner. When the ruffle is completely pinned, place the backing fabric, face down, on top of this, matching the raw edges (photograph 6). Sew the front and back of the pillow together, catching the ruffle in the seam and stitching ½ inch in from the raw edges. Leave a 10-inch opening (Figure B); trim the corners, and turn the pillow cover right side out. Insert a pillow form or fill the cover with loose stuffing. Stitch the opening closed by hand.

Needlecrafts
Parquet ribbon pillow

$ ☒ 🚶 🧵

Rich-looking velvets and boldly patterned grosgrain ribbons are combined in this parquet pillow, designed to form an angular pattern like that of a parquet floor.

Parquet pattern adds interest to wood floors by providing an angular design. The same is true of the parquet ribbon pillow, pictured above. The geometric design is surprisingly easy to make. For the 18-inch-square pillow, you will need: ½ yard of 45-inch-wide backing fabric for the ribbons; a 19-inch square of fabric for the back of the pillow cover; thread; an 18-inch knife-edge pillow form, or loose stuffing of polyester fiber; and ribbon. The total amount of ribbon you need will depend on the width used. You will need 40 inches of each ribbon; their widths should total 10 inches.

To start the pillow, cut a 10-by-40-inch rectangle from the ribbon-backing fabric. Starting ¼ inch in from one long edge of the fabric, stitch the ribbons to the fabric along their long edges, being careful not to leave any space between them. The result is a 40-inch strip of ribbon-covered fabric (photograph 7, opposite). This will be cut and arranged to form the parquet design.

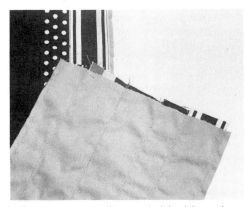

7: To start parquet pillows, stitch both long edges of 40-inch-long ribbons to the backing fabric. Place the ribbons close to each other so no backing fabric shows.

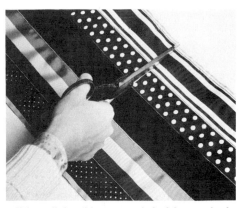

8: When all the ribbons are stitched down on both long edges, cut the 40-inch strip into four 10-inch squares, thus making the four smaller squares that will form the pillow front.

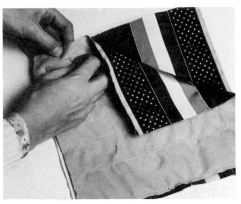

9: Place two of the squares, right sides facing, so the ribbons are at right angles to each other. Pin and stitch ½ inch in from one raw edge. Repeat with the other two squares; press the seams open.

Cut the strip into four 10-inch squares (photograph 8). Choose either of the edge ribbons to be the center ribbon, forming a cross in the middle of the pillow. In this pillow, the ribbon with small polka dots was chosen. Place two of the squares, right sides together, so the ribbons are at right angles to each other and the chosen ribbon forms the inside angle (photograph 9). Stitch these two squares together ½ inch from the edge of the fabric. Repeat with the other two squares. To press the seams open, use a steam iron and a pressing cloth. Iron on the wrong side. If you have used any velvet ribbon, be careful not to press over it as the iron will leave a permanent mark on velvet. Place the two resulting rectangles together, right sides facing, so the ribbons opposite each other are at right angles and the chosen ribbon is on the inside. Pin this seam, matching the center seams of the rectangles (photograph 10). Stitch ½ inch in from the edge of the fabric. Press the seam open.

To finish the pillow, cut the material for the back of the cover into a 19-inch square. Place this on top of the parquet ribbon design, matching the edges, with right sides facing. Stitch them together ½ inch from the edge, leaving a 10-inch opening along one edge. To square off the corners, pull the front and back of the pillow cover apart so the two side seams that form one corner lie on top of each other (Figure C), and stitch in toward the center 1 inch from the corner, over the side seams. Repeat with the other three corners. Trim the corners, and turn the pillow cover right side out; fill with a pillow form or with stuffing. Stitch the opening closed, making small stitches by hand.

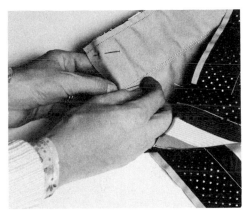

10: Pin the two ribbon rectangles together, right sides facing, matching the center seams. Make sure the ribbons all meet at right angles to each other. Stitch ½ inch in from the edge and press the seam open.

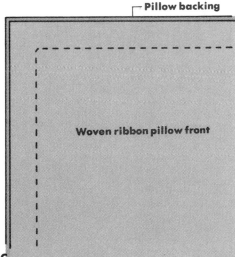

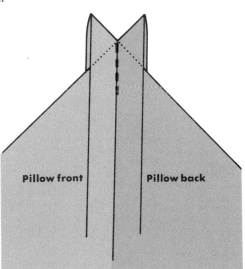

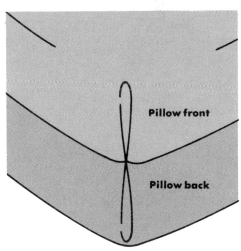

Figure C: To make a square corner with a tuck, bring the seams of the corner (left) together by pulling front and back apart. Open the seam allowance, and stitch 1 inch down from the corner point (center) on top of the seams. Repeat on all four corners. Turn right side out; the corners will be squared off with tucks (right).

Patchwork and ribbon pillow

The combination of patchwork fabric with woven ribbons makes a pillow with an old-country look.

The ever-popular art of patchwork can be combined with the woven-ribbon technique to make an interesting pillow cover. If you have scraps of fabric left from other sewing projects, a pillow cover like the one pictured above is inexpensive to make. You will need: twenty-five 4-inch squares of various fabrics, and ¾ yard of fabric for the ruffle; ½ yard of fabric for the back cover; ½ yard each of eight different ribbons (a total of 4 yards) for the front cover of the pillow; thread; and a 15-inch-square knife-edge pillow form or loose stuffing.

11: To make patchwork pillow fabric, pin two 4-inch squares, right sides facing, and sew them ½ inch in from one raw edge. Repeat until you have five rows of five squares each. Press the seams open, and stitch the rows together.

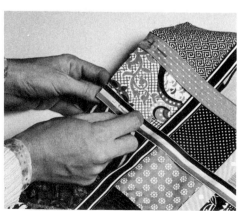

12: Place vertical and horizontal ribbons over the patchwork seams. Pin them in place at the top and left ends only, so the free ends can be woven together.

13: Weave the first horizontal ribbon over the first vertical ribbon, under the second, and so forth. Weave the second horizontal ribbon in the opposite way. Repeat with remaining ribbons.

To make the 15-inch-square pillow cover, start with the patchwork background. Pin two squares together, right sides facing, and stitch ½ inch in from one edge (photograph 11). (The 4-inch squares allow a ½-inch seam; each finished piece will be 3 inches square.) Continue joining squares until you have five squares in a row. Make five rows of five squares each and press the seams open. Join the rows matching the interior seams. Press these seams open and you will have a 16-inch square made of 25 smaller ones.

Weaving the Ribbons

The ribbons, placed on top of the patchwork seams, are interwoven. Cut each ribbon 16 inches long. Pin the ribbons (one end only) on top of the seams in the patchwork, with four ribbons running vertically and four running horizontally (photograph 12). Flip the horizontal ribbons to the side of the patchwork and weave them under and over the vertical ribbons (photograph 13). Pin the opposite end of each ribbon in place after weaving it. When all the ribbons are in place, sew them to the patchwork fabric by stitching ¼ inch in from all edges of the fabric. For directions on how to make and attach the ruffle, see page 1765.

To finish the pillow cover, cut out a 16-inch square of fabric for the back cover. Place this on top of the ribbon-patchwork square, right sides facing. Stitch around the square ½ inch in from the edge, leaving a 10-inch opening. Trim the corners, and turn the pillow cover right side out. Insert a pillow form or stuff with polyester fiber. Close the opening by making small stitches by hand.

Needlecrafts
Tennis racket cover $ ☒ ☗ ✄

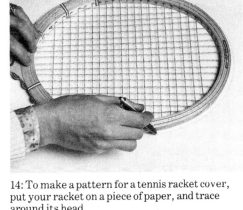

14: To make a pattern for a tennis racket cover, put your racket on a piece of paper, and trace around its head.

Woven-ribbon fabric is not limited to home decoration; it can be put to unusual uses, as in the tennis racket cover pictured on page 1770. To make the woven-ribbon cover, you will need: ½ yard of polyester-and-cotton fabric to back the ribbons; ½ yard of color-coordinated fabric for the zippered back cover; a 12-inch zipper; ⅞-inch-wide bias-tape binding; and ribbon. To determine the amount of ribbon needed, measure the length and width of the head of your racket; the ribbons will be woven on a rectangle that has the same measurements as the racket head. (The racket pictured measured 12 by 17 inches.) Cut a piece of polyester-and-cotton fabric to this size and weave the ribbons over it, following the directions given on page 1765.

To make a pattern for the tennis racket cover, place the racket on a piece of paper, and trace around its head (photograph 14). Add ¼ inch around the edge for a seam allowance. Cut out this paper pattern, and pin it to the woven-ribbon rectangle (photograph 15). With the pattern pinned on, stitch around it 1/16 inch out-

15: Add ¼ inch around the outer edge of the paper pattern to allow for a seam allowance. Then cut out the pattern and pin it to the rectangle of woven ribbons.

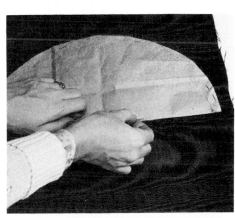

16: To make the back of the racket cover, fold the pattern in half, and pin it to a double thickness of fabric, allowing ½ inch extra at the center fold for the zipper seam.

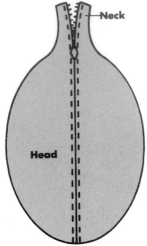

D

Figure D: Following package directions, insert the zipper in the seam at the center of the back, making sure the top of the zipper is at hanhandle opening.

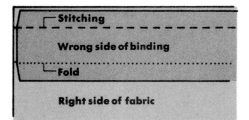

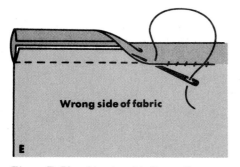

E

Figure E: Place bias-tape binding on the neck opening with right sides together; stitch along the first fold line (top). Fold the binding to the back of the racket cover, and stitch the second fold to the fabric by hand (bottom). Bias-tape binding is also used to join the edges of the back and front pieces.

A fashionable way to protect a tennis racket is with a woven-ribbon cover, designed to harmonize with a tennis dress.

side the pattern edge. This will secure the woven ribbons to the backing fabric. Then cut out the shape just outside the stitching, and remove the paper pattern.

To make the back cover, fold the paper pattern in half, and place it on a double thickness of the back cover fabric (photograph 16). Pin the pattern in place and cut the fabric, allowing ½ inch extra along the fold line for a seam. Stitch this seam in the center back of the racket cover, and put in the zipper, following the package directions. Make sure that the opening at the top of the zipper is at the neck of the racket cover (Figure D). Before stitching the front and back covers together, finish the raw edges of both pieces at the neck opening with bias-tape binding. With right sides together, place the opened binding on top of the neck opening. Stitch the binding to the fabric along the first fold line (Figure E, top). Turn the binding to the inside of the fabric, and stitch the second fold to the fabric by hand (Figure E, bottom). To complete the racket cover, place the front on the back, with wrong sides facing. Pin the opened bias-tape binding on the racket cover front and stitch along the first fold going through all three layers—the front, the back, and the binding. Thus, stitching the front and back together and attaching the binding are accomplished in one operation. Fold the binding to the back, and stitch it to the back of the cover by hand.

Needlecrafts
Ribbon evening bag

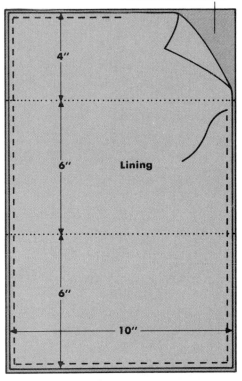

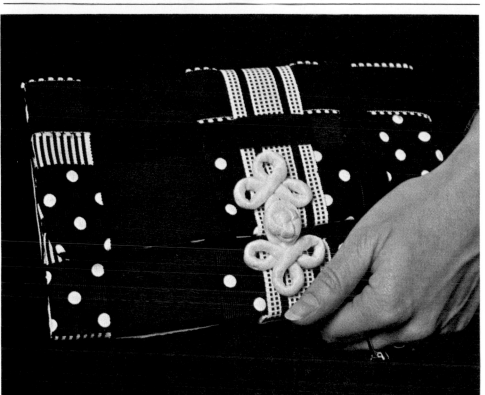

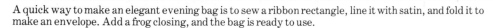

A quick way to make an elegant evening bag is to sew a ribbon rectangle, line it with satin, and fold it to make an envelope. Add a frog closing, and the bag is ready to use.

Ribbon clutch bags make luxurious evening accessories. They are easy to make and inexpensive, so you can have several to complement your favorite evening dresses. One option is basic black, such as the bag shown above. It measures 6 by 10 inches when folded and is made from a 10-by-16-inch rectangle of woven ribbons. The bottom part of the bag is turned up and stitched at the sides to form the carrying pocket. A frog closing, available in department stores or sewing supply stores, completes the bag.

To make the evening bag, you will need: ½ yard of polyester-and-cotton fabric for backing the ribbons; ½ yard of satin for the lining; thread; a frog closing in a color that harmonizes with the ribbons; and ribbons. The amount of ribbon needed depends on the width used. You will need 17-inch lengths of ribbon whose combined width totals 11 inches, and 11-inch lengths of ribbon whose combined width totals 17 inches.

Cut an 11-by-17-inch rectangle of backing fabric, and cut as many lengths of ribbon as you need according to the width of the ribbons you use. Weave the ribbons following the directions for the woven-ribbon pillow on page 1765. Cut an 11-by-17-inch rectangle of satin lining, and stitch it to the woven-ribbon rectangle, using a ½-inch seam margin and keeping the right sides together. Leave a 6-inch opening along one side. Trim the corners, and turn the bag right side out. Press the bag on the lined side, using a steam iron and a pressing cloth to protect the ribbons. Avoid ironing any velvet ribbon. Stitch the opening closed by hand.

With the bag face down, turn up the bottom 6 inches to form a pocket (Figure F). Taking small stitches by hand, sew the sides closed. Fold the top down to form the flap. Stitch one part of the frog closing to the center of the bottom edge of the flap and the corresponding part to the center of the bag. For an alternate closing, sew a button to the center of the bag, and stitch a ribbon loop to the center of the edge of the flap.

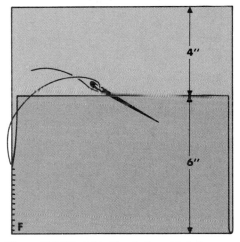

Figure F: With right sides facing, stitch the lining of the evening bag to the ribbon rectangle ½ inch in from the raw edge (top). To form a pocket, place the bag face down, fold the bottom 6 inches up, and stitch the sides together (bottom).

Needlecrafts
Beribboned serving tray

$ ☒ 👫 🎨

The clear plastic top of this serving tray lets the beauty of ribbons show through, while protecting them from spills. The ribbons are arranged and glued on a piece of poster board that has been cut to the same size as the clear plastic top.

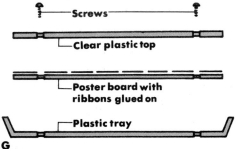

G

Figure G: To assemble a ribbon tray, place ribbon-covered posterboard on top of the tray bottom; then put clear plastic on top, and hold it in place with screws.

The serving tray pictured is a simple way to decorate with ribbons that requires no sewing. Ribbon, white household glue, and poster board are used. The tray, made of opaque acrylic plastic, has a separate clear plastic top piece that protects the design. The trays are sold at needlework shops.

To make the ribbon design, remove the clear plastic top piece for the tray, and trace around it on the poster board. Cut out the outlined area; this rectangle is the exact size of the finished design and serves as the backing for the ribbons. Form your own designs with ribbons on the poster board rectangle. When you are pleased with the design, glue the ribbons in place. Place the ribbons so woven edges cover cut edges; then no raw edges will show. Let the glue dry for at least an hour. Put the clear plastic piece on top of the ribbon design, and mark the poster board to indicate where the four screws will go. Make a small hole at each mark so the screws do not tear the ribbons. Put the layers together, and insert the screws (Figure G). The clear plastic top shows off your handwork while protecting it from spills.

Needlecrafts
Blooming T-shirt

¢ ☒ 🧍 🎨

A bucket woven of ribbons and filled with fabric flowers adorns the front of what was an ordinary T-shirt (pictured opposite). With such appliques you can transform any shirt or sweater. You might use the flower color to coordinate an outfit, or simply cut the flowers out of scraps of fabric you like. The pattern for the flowers and the bucket (Figure H) can be made in any size you want; a large version might suit the back of a sweater and a smaller version might be better for a child's shirt.

To make the bucket, decide on the size that you want, and cut a piece of backing fabric to the width of the bucket at its base and the height of the bucket at its cen-

You do not need to have a green thumb to make the fabric flowers bloom on a T-shirt.

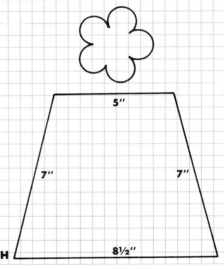

Figure H: To enlarge the flower and bucket shapes, draw a grid to the size that you want, and transfer the designs square by square.

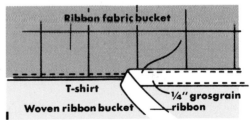

Figure I: To secure the woven-ribbon bucket to the T shirt, place ½-inch-wide ribbon over the raw edges, and stitch along both edges of the ribbon.

ter. Weave the ribbons on this backing fabric, following the directions for the woven pillow on page 1765. Enlarge the trapezoid pattern (Figure H), and place it on top of the woven-ribbon rectangle. Stitch around the pattern 1/16 inch outside its edge. Remove the pattern, and trim the ribbons ⅛ inch outside the stitching. Enlarge the flower pattern and cut as many flowers as you want.

Arrange the flowers and the bucket on your shirt, and pin them in place. Border the flowers with a satin stitch, either using your sewing machine or stitching by hand, thus securing the flowers to the shirt. Secure the bucket to the shirt by stitching ½-inch-wide ribbon over the edges (Figure I). To make a ribbon handle, stitch a piece of ribbon at the top of the bucket and at the top of the flowers. For related crafts and projects, see "Applique," "Machine Stitchery," "Patchwork," and "Tablet and Frame Weaving."

Motion That Soothes

Making things has been both hobby and business for Jackson Hand, writer and photographer, for more than 30 years. He has been home workshop editor for Better Homes & Gardens, *home improvement editor for* McCall's, *consulting editor in home improvement for* Popular Science, *and consultant for a book on home repairs published by Time-Life Books,* How Things Work in Your Home (and what to do when they don't). *Among the books Jackson has written are* How to Do Your Own Wood Finishing, How to Do Your Own Painting and Papering, *and* The Complete Book of Home Repairs & Maintenance.

The rocking chairs made by Shaker craftsmen in the eighteenth century are notable for their light weight, pure lines, and acorn-or pine-cone-shaped finials atop the back posts. At first, seats were made of woven rush or splint, later of fabric tapes. Originally designed for the use of the aged or infirm Shakers, these chairs became treasures sought by other Americans as early as the 1800s.

A Boston rocker of typical nineteenth-century design has the spindle back and angled legs characteristic of the Windsor chair from which it was derived. But the rolling seat lines, curved arms and large headpiece (frequently stenciled) identify it as a Boston rocker.

Perhaps the child is father to the man. The history of cradles and rockers seems to confirm it. Rocking cradles existed for centuries before the first rocking chair for adult use was made in colonial America. Rocking toys, like the horse used by young King Charles I (opposite, lower right), were amusing English children before the first English colonists sailed for the New World.

No one knows the name of the inventive American who first gave a rocking motion to an adult chair. It was not, as has been reported, Benjamin Franklin, though he did own one. Nor was the idea entirely fresh—rocking chairs for children were made in England before the first American rocker appeared.

Stubby Carpet Cutters

During the early 1700s, cabinetmakers in colonial America produced many cradles and cribs that had curved runners attached for rocking. About the middle of the century, they began putting curved runners on adult chairs. Because these runners were fitted into notches cut into the legs of an existing chair, they had to be quite narrow—so narrow they were called carpet cutters. The first runners also tended to be stubby, extending only a little way beyond the front and back legs of the chair. Only later—probably after a number of colonists had flipped while rocking—did cabinetmakers learn to improve the balance (and save the carpets) by using broad runners that extended farther at the rear than at the front.

One way to estimate the age of an antique rocker is to check the length of the runners extending in the rear. If they extend more than 6 inches, the chair is probably not one of the earliest rockers. But if the rear extension is quite short, the runners are narrow, and the side rails of the chair are close to the runners, you may have a real find—one of the first chairs converted for rocking in the 1700s.

From the beginning, rocking chairs were made for relaxing. They were functional rather than decorative, and often had a classic simplicity typified by the rockers made by the Shakers (top left). Later, rocker designs became more elaborate as cabinetmakers put rockers on other chair designs that were popular. A favorite was the Windsor, a sturdy, lightweight chair with a back made of spindles that earned it the name of stick chair. The Windsor design with runners added was the prototype of a famous rocking chair—the Boston rocker (bottom, left).

Leather Ears and Real Horsehair

As the Americans prospered, they did not forget the children. Rocking toys and cradles became more elaborately structured and detailed. The primitive boat-shaped rocking horses used in King Charles's time were replaced with realistically carved and painted horses on runners. They had ears and reins of leather, manes and tails of real horsehair, as in the painting opposite. Rocking cradles also grew fancier; simple pine cradles were succeeded by cradles with spindled sides and lathe-turned corner posts.

The projects detailed here hark back to where the idea of rockers originated—with the children. The child's rocking chair (page 1776) is a simple modern version of the small rocker used by children of seventeenth-century England. The rocker boat (page 1777) is reminiscent of the early boat-shaped rocking horses. The infant's cradle of pine boards (page 1779) follows a typical early American design. And the spindle-sided doll's cradle with turned corner posts (page 1780) represents a more prosperous period in American life, when even a doll could have elaborate decorative furniture.

All four can be built with hand tools, as were the originals that inspired them, although the turned spindles on the doll's cradle were purchased ready-made at a lumberyard. You will need: crosscut saw; coping or keyhole saw; drill with ⅜-, ½-, ¾-, 1-inch, and countersink bits; wood rasp or plane; coarse and fine sandpaper; all-purpose white glue; string; and a pencil. The wood, fasteners, and finishes needed are listed with each project.

A Massachusetts artist, now unknown, painted the portrait above, showing two children with their hobby horse—about 1840. The realistic and elaborately detailed rocking horse, with a mane and tail of real horsehair, contrasts with the rough-hewn wooden rocking horse shown at right, below, used by King Charles I of England when he was a young boy early in the seventeenth century. Boat-shaped rockers characterized early rocking horses.

A 17-month-old youngster finds this rocking chair just about the right size for him. For an older child, you may need to increase the enlargement scale suggested in Figure A.

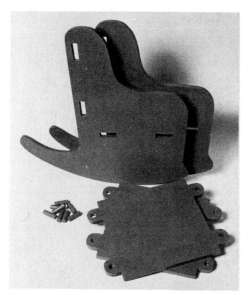

1: Two matching sides and a matching seat and back make the chair. These parts are locked together with short pieces of dowel.

Furniture and Finishes
Child's rocking chair

A 4-by-4-foot sheet of ½-inch plywood and eight 1-inch lengths of ½-inch dowel went into the sturdy red rocking chair pictured at left. The cut-out parts and dowels are shown in photograph 1. The extension ears or tabs on the seat and back slip through the slots on the sides and are held in place with dowel pins (photograph 2). This form of construction, known as locked tenon joinery, lets you put the chair together in minutes, or take it apart just as quickly for carrying or storage.

For the chair sides, cut two 19-inch squares of plywood. Stack these so their edges match; then tack them together with small nails. This will hold them while you cut out both pieces at once. Enlarge the pattern for the sides (Figure A), and with carbon paper, transfer it onto the plywood. Then saw out the side shapes, using a coping or a keyhole saw. (A power saber saw, of course, is faster.) To make the ½-by-1¾-inch slots, four in each side, drill ½-inch holes at the ends of each slot; then saw the slots out (photograph 3). Square off the corners with a coping saw or a small flat rasp.

For the matching seat and back, cut two 10-by-13-inch rectangles of plywood, and tack them together as you did the sides. Enlarge the pattern for these pieces (Figure A), transfer the pattern to the stacked pieces, and saw them out. Make sure each hole you have traced on an extension ear is exactly ½ inch out from the adjacent edge, so the pin will fit snugly against the side piece when the ear is in its slot. If not, redraw the hole with a compass, marking the center ¾ inches out from the edge. Then drill the holes with a ½-inch bit.

Separate the stacked pieces, remove the nails, fill their holes with wood plastic, and sand each part on all sides with 120-grit, then 220-grit sandpaper. Cut eight ½-inch dowels 1 inch long and sand the ends. Slip the ears of the seat and the back through the slots in the sides to make sure everything fits. Then disassemble, and give each piece a prime coat of shellac-base sealer. Finish with semigloss enamel. When this has dried, slip the pieces together, and tap the dowels in place.

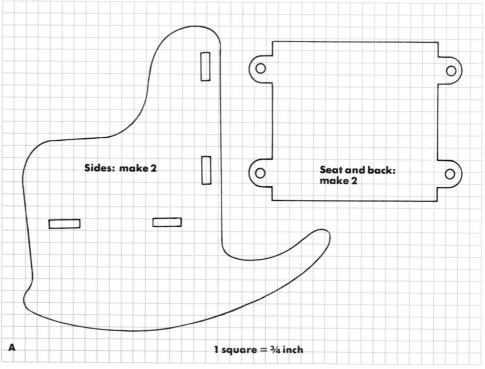

Sides: make 2

Seat and back: make 2

A   1 square = ¾ inch

Figure A: To enlarge these patterns for the chair sides and the seat and back, draw a grid of ¾-inch squares on a piece of paper, and copy the pattern lines (including the slots in the sides and the holes in the seat and back tabs) one square at a time. Then with carbon paper, transfer the enlarged pattern to the plywood.

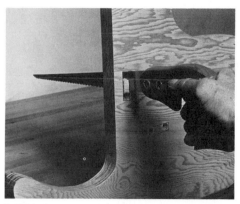

2: This method of locking the seat and back to the sides of the chair—with tabs and dowels—lets you assemble the chair or take it apart quickly. It is known as locked tenon joinery.

3: With the cut-out side pieces fastened together, drill holes at the ends of the slots; then cut out the slots with a keyhole saw. Square up the corners with a small rasp.

In a modern adaptation of the rocking horse of young King Charles I, this young man goes for a rollicking cruise rather than a gallop. His ship is a safe one that he cannot capsize.

Toys and Games
Rocker boat

Unless they live on the range, modern children are more likely to encounter boats than horses. So in a rocker ship (right, above) the bounding main is substituted for the open range while retaining the boat-shaped rockers used on seventeenth-century rocking horses (page 1775).

To make the rocker ship you will need: two pieces of 1-by-10-inch pine, 32⅜ inches long for the sides; two pieces of 1-by-4-inch pine, 14 inches long for the uprights; two pieces of 1-by-4-inch pine, 16½ inches long for the end pieces (the reason for the extra width will become apparent); one piece of 1-by-6-inch pine, 6½ inches long for the seat; two pieces of ¾-by-¾-by-5¼-inch pine for the seat cleats; one piece of 1-inch dowel, 15⅜ inches long for the handle; one piece of ¼-inch plywood, 18 inches wide by 40 inches long for the bottom; 24 No. 8 flathead wood screws, 1¼ inches long; all-purpose white glue; and semigloss enamels. Figure B shows how the parts of the ship go together.

To make the curved bottoms of the rockers, stack the two long pieces of 1-by-10-inch pine, and tack them together temporarily with small nails. Enlarge the pattern for the sides (Figure C), transfer it to the stacked pieces so the top lines up with an edge, and saw out the bottom curves with a coping or keyhole saw. Separate the stacked pieces, remove the nails, and fill their holes—and any holes in the straight plywood edge—with wood plastic. Sand the cut edges smooth with coarse and then fine sandpaper.

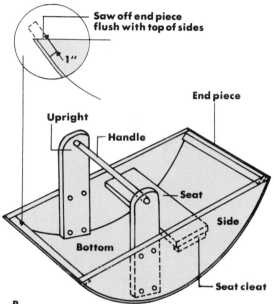

B
Figure B: The parts of the rocker ship are fitted together as illustrated above. The end pieces are fitted between the sides, then are sawed off flush with the tops of the side pieces, as the detail drawing shows.

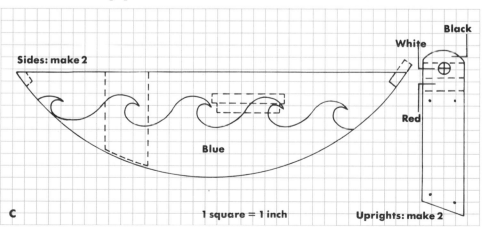

Figure C: To enlarge these patterns for the ship sides and the uprights, rule a sheet of paper into 1-inch squares. Then copy the design (including the patterns for waves and the smokestack bands) one square at a time, transferring the lines from the small grid above to the larger grid you have made.

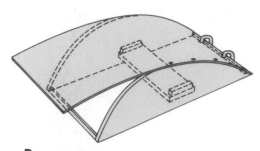

D

Figure D: After you have applied glue to one end piece and the tips of the adjacent side pieces, clamp the plywood bottom in place and screw it down. Then bend the plywood around the rockers, gluing and screwing it in place as you go.

Next fasten the end pieces between the two sides using glue and 1¼-inch flathead wood screws, countersinking the screw heads. Saw off the top of each end piece flush with the sides (detail, Figure B, page 1777). Glue and screw the seat cleats in position on each side, and mount the seat on top of these cleats (Figures B and C, page 1777).

You now have the basic frame of the rocker ship, with the sides held together by the end pieces and the seat. To attach the plywood bottom, turn the frame upside down so it rests on the flat top edges of the rockers. Put glue on the front of one of the end pieces, and clamp one end of the 18-by-40-inch piece of ¼-inch plywood to this piece so it is flush with the edges of the end and side pieces (Figure D). Screw the plywood to the end piece and the tips of the sides using No. 8 flathead wood screws, 1 inch long, placed ⅜ inch from either edge and spaced about 1⅞ inches apart. Then, applying glue to the curved edge of the rockers as you go, bend the plywood around the rockers, and fasten it with No. 8 flathead wood screws 1¼ inches long spaced about 4 inches apart. Drill pilot holes for the screws, and countersink the heads below the surface of the plywood. It helps if you drive a screw first on one side, then on the other as you go.

When you reach the other end of the curve, put glue on the end piece, clamp it, then screw it on as you did the first end. Saw off the plywood flush with the end and side pieces.

Stack the two pieces—1-by-4-inch pine, 14 inches long—that will form the uprights, and fasten them together temporarily with small nails. Enlarge the pattern for the uprights (Figure C, page 1777), and trace it on the stacked pieces. Cut out the uprights, and drill the hole for the 1-inch dowel handle. Put glue on the ends of the dowel handle and in the holes in the uprights. Then slip the dowel handle in place. Fasten the uprights to the sides with two screws at the bottom and two near the top of each side (Figure B, page 1777).

Sand all sharp edges with coarse, then fine sandpaper. With wood plastic fill in the holes over the countersunk screws, and sand smooth. The ship's color is for you to choose but don't forget to put bands of color on the uprights (so they look like ship's funnels) and blue waves on the sides of the boat. If you plan to use the boat outdoors, apply two coats of exterior enamel.

Furniture and Finishes

Infant's rocking cradle

Early American craftsmen, working with simple tools and soft pine wood, made charming furniture pieces like the rocking cradle pictured opposite. It consists of two ends, two sides, a board bottom, and strips to support the bottom (Figure E). If you can find two 17-by-24-inch pieces of 1-inch pine, one end of the cradle can be cut from each. But a more practical and economical solution is to cut each end from two glued-together pieces of pine, as in Figure F.

To do this, you will need a 10-foot length of 1-by-12-inch pine and a 6-foot length of 1-by-6-inch pine. You also need a board ¾ by 12⅝ by 29⅛ inches for the bottom. Do not be concerned if the wood has some knots or blemishes in it; such character marks will make it look like the wood used in early American furniture.

From the 10-foot piece, cut two 24-inch lengths and two 30-inch lengths. Cut two 16-inch lengths from the 1-by-6. Edge-glue a 16-inch piece of 1-by-6 to each of the 24-inch lengths of 1-by-12, centering the shorter piece exactly on the longer piece as in Figure F. If you have a pipe clamp or bar clamp or can borrow one, use it to hold the two pieces together until the glue is dry; if not, clamp with rope or buckled straps drawn tightly around the two pieces. When the glue has dried, stack the end pieces and fasten them together temporarily with small nails.

Next enlarge the pattern for the ends (Figure G), and transfer it onto the wood using carbon paper. Saw out the end shapes, using a crosscut saw for straight cuts and a coping or keyhole saw for the curved lines. With a ¾-inch bit, drill a hole at each end of the pattern marked for the handholds; then cut out the handholds with a coping or keyhole saw. Separate the stacked pieces, remove the nails, and fill the nail holes with wood plastic.

Bottom supports

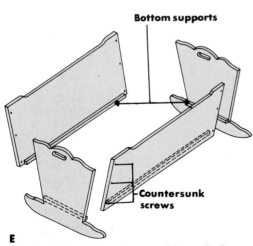

Countersunk screws

E

Figure E: Here is how the parts of the cradle fit together. Strips glued and nailed to the ends and side support the removable bottom, not shown here.

Baby nestles in a rocking cradle of pine boards similar to those made by colonial craftsmen.

Figure F: To make a piece of solid pine large enough for the ends of the cradle, edge-glue two pieces of standard-width lumber together as shown. (Do not place the joint where the rocker joins the end.)

The two 30-inch pieces of 1-by-12 form the sides of the cradle. They can be shaped as in Figure G or left with straight tops. To shape them, stack the pieces, and fasten them together temporarily with small nails. Enlarge the pattern for the sides (Figure G), and transfer it onto the wood with carbon paper. Cut the curved top outline with a coping or keyhole saw. Separate the stacked pieces, remove the nails, and fill the nail holes with wood plastic.

Fasten the sides to the ends with glue and No. 8 flathead wood screws 1½ inches long (Figure E), countersinking the heads and filling the holes with wood plastic. (If you have the patience, you can make the piece look more authentically early American by drilling ¼ inch down into each screw hole and gluing short sections of dowel into these holes after the screws have been driven in.)

From the leftover piece of 1-by-6, cut two strips ¾ by ¾ by 28¾ inches for the bottom supports on the sides, and two strips ¾ by ¾ by 12⅜ inches for the bottom supports on the ends; these overlap the side supports. Glue and screw these supports to the ends and sides (Figure E), drilling and countersinking for No. 8 flathead wood screws 1¼ inches long. With a plane or rasp bevel the sides of the bottom board until they match the slope of the sides of the cradle. Try resting the bottom on the supports to make sure it will fit and can easily be removed for cleaning.

Use a rasp or coarse sandpaper to round all edges, then fine sandpaper to make them smooth. Much pine furniture made by early American craftsmen had no finish. Gradually it aged to a dark brown. You can simulate that aged look by wiping on a pigmented stain of a suitable color. You may want to give the bottom board two or three coats of enamel so it will be easy to clean.

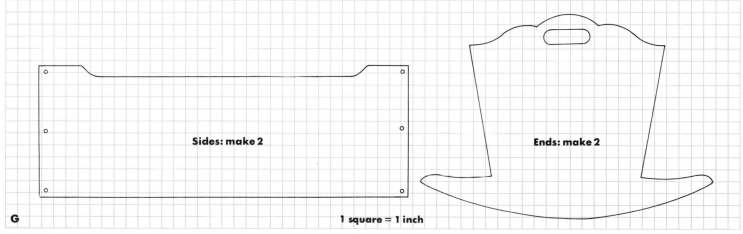

Sides: make 2

Ends: make 2

G   1 square = 1 inch

Figure G: Enlarge these patterns for the ends and sides of the cradle on paper that you have ruled into 1-inch squares. Copy the designs (including the handholds) one square at a time from the small grid above to the larger grid you have made.

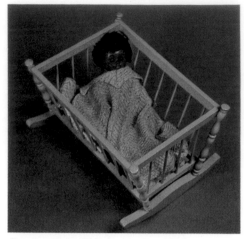

Construction of this fancy doll cradle is made easier by the fact that the turned corner posts are available as stock items at lumberyards.

Toys and Games
Doll's cradle

Ready-turned spindles you can buy at lumberyards make this cradle a lot simpler to build than it seems at first glance. These and other components are shown in photograph 5. You will need: two pieces of 1-by-2 inch pine, 15 inches long, and two pieces of 1-by-2 inch pine, 10⅛ inches long for the top and bottom end rails; four pieces of 1-by-2 inch pine, 22¼ inches long for the top and bottom side rails; two pieces of 2-by-4 inch pine, 20 inches long for the rockers; one piece of ¼-inch plywood, 9¾ by 20⅝ inches for the bottom; four strips of ¼-inch-square wood—two of them 9½ inches long and two of them 20¼ inches long—to support the bottom; eight ⅜-inch dowels, 9½ inches long for the end spindles; and fourteen ⅜-inch dowels, 9¾ inches long for the side spindles; four turned spindles about 15 inches long for the corner posts; four wooden drawer pulls to serve as finials on top of the corner posts; eight No. 8 flathead wood screws, 1¾ inches long; eight No. 8 flathead wood screws, 1¼ inches long; all-purpose white glue; several small nails; and some wood plastic.

First you cut and assemble the side and end rails and spindles that form the

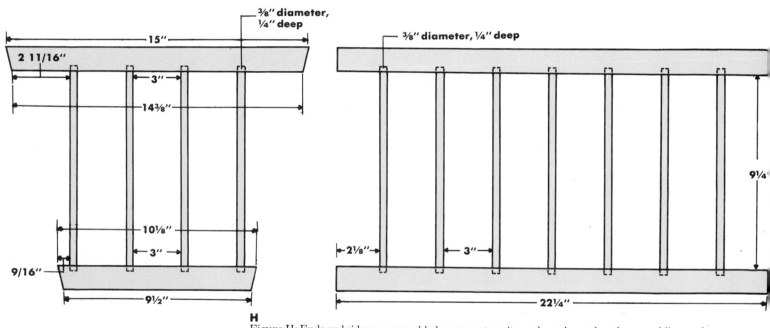

H

Figure H: Ends and sides are assembled as separate units as shown here; then the assemblies are fastened together where the rails meet at the corners. This forms the inner frame of the cradle.

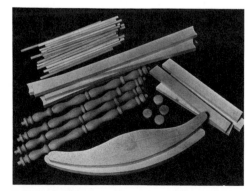

5: Dowels, drawer pulls, readymade turned spindles (for corner posts), and side and end rails and rockers cut from standard lumber were used to make the doll cradle.

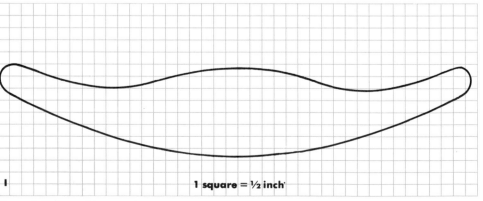

Figure I: Enlarge this pattern for the cradle rockers on paper that you have ruled into ½-inch squares. Copy the design one square at a time, transferring the lines from the small grid above to the larger grid you have made.

inner frame of the cradle (Figure H). Cut the ends of the 10⅛-inch-long bottom end rails at an angle so that their bottoms measure 9½ inches (sloping in 5/16 inch at each end). Cut the 15-inch-long top end rails at an angle so that their bottoms measure 14⅜ inches (sloping in 5/16 inch at each end). These angled cuts establish the slope of the cradle sides.

Assembling Side and End Rails

Starting 2⅛ inches from one end of each top and bottom side rail, drill ⅜-inch-diameter holes ¼ inch deep and spaced 3 inches apart, center to center, for the seven dowel spindles that will fit between each pair of side rails. Starting 9/16 inch from one end of each bottom end rail, drill ⅜-inch-diameter holes ¼ inch deep and spaced 3 inches apart, center to center, for the four dowel spindles that will fit between each pair of top and bottom end rails. Make sure these holes are drilled into the longer (10⅛-inch side) of the bottom end rails. Drill corresponding holes into the underside (14⅜-inch side) of the top end rails, starting 2 11/16 inches in from one end and spacing the holes 3 inches apart, center to center. Glue seven 9¾-inch-long dowels into each pair of side rails and four 9½-inch-long dowels into each pair of end rails. Then glue and nail the side rails to the end rails to form the inner frame of the cradle. Set this assembly aside while you make the rockers.

For the rockers, stack the two 20-inch-long pieces of 2-by-4 inch pine, wide sides facing, and fasten them together temporarily with small nails. Then enlarge the pattern for the rockers (Figure I), and transfer it to the wood. Saw out the rocker curves with a keyhole saw, remove the nails, and separate the pieces.

Fitting Corner Posts and Rockers

Set the assembled cradle frame on end with one set of end rails facing up at working height. Lay a turned corner post along one side, centering it on the ends of a pair of side rails. Adjust it until the turned portion of the post (not including the tip that will fit into the rocker) is 1⅛ inches below the bottom of the lower rail (Figure J). Drive nails through the center of the turned post part way into the top and bottom side rail to hold the post in this position temporarily. Where the turning meets a side rail, pencil a matching curve onto the end of the side rail so you can shape the end for a snug fit after the post has been removed. The top of the turned corner post should be marked where you will saw it off just above the top rail. A drawer pull glued at this point will give the post a finished appearance. Follow the same procedure with a second corner post at the opposite corner.

Center one of the rockers under the projecting tips of the two corner posts, holding it so the tips extend over the rocker as in Figure J. With a pencil trace around these tips to fix the angle and position for holes in the rocker, into which the tips will fit. Remove the rocker, extend the side lines up over its top, and drill holes to receive the corner post tips in the top of the rocker. Remove the two corner posts you fastened temporarily to the side rails, saw off the tops as marked, and glue their lower tips into the drilled holes. Then use a half-round rasp to shape the ends of the side rails to match the curvature of the turning.

Upend the inner frame and repeat the procedure so you have a second set of rockers joined to turned posts on the opposite end of the cradle.

Glue the drawer pulls to the tops of the corner posts; then mount the corner post and rocker assemblies on each end of the cradle. Drill pilot holes; then attach the posts using glue and No. 8 flathead screws 1¾ inches long, countersinking the heads below the surface (Figure K). Glue and nail the ¼-inch-square strips that support the cradle bottom inside the bottom edge of the side rails and end rails. Since the side rails tilt upward slightly, you may want to bevel the top of the side rails slightly with sandpaper or the rasp so the bottom will rest evenly on both side and end supporting strips. Try the plywood bottom to make sure it will fit and can be removed easily for cleaning.

There will be some gaps where the turned corner posts meet the side rails and the bottom rockers. Fill these with wood plastic, as well as the countersunk holes of the corner screws. Round all sharp edges slightly with coarse sandpaper; then smooth all parts with fine sandpaper. The cradle can be painted quickly with spray enamel.

For related entries, see "Preschool Projects," "Table Games," "Toys."

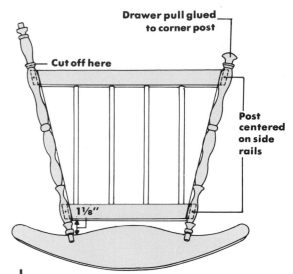

Drawer pull glued to corner post

Cut off here

Post centered on side rails

1⅛"

J

Figure J: With nails temporarily fasten the corner posts to the side rails. Then hold a rocker under the tips of the corner posts, and trace around these tips to establish the location and angle of the holes you will drill for the tips in the rocker. Mark the top of the corner post so you can trim it off close to the top rail; then add a drawer-pull finial, as at right.

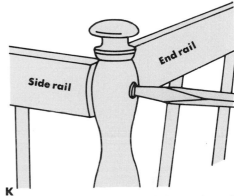

Side rail

End rail

K

Figure K: After corner posts have been trimmed and drawer pulls added to their tops, and corner post tips glued into the rockers, fasten the corner posts to each side rail using countersunk screws.

ROPE KNOTTING
Craft of the Ancient Mariner

Knowing how to tie a few basic knots makes anyone's life run more smoothly. If you can expeditiously tie up a package or a bundle of old newspapers to be recycled, or tie a lure to a fishing line, a boat to a dock, a tent to a stake, a rose to a trellis, many of your knotty problems will disappear. In fact, with only a bit of practice you can use knots to make such decorative accessories as wall hangings, belts, place mats, napkin rings, and hanging planters.

My knowledge of knots began when I first went to sea at the age of 17, more than 40 years ago. At an earlier time, a sailor's life depended on the strength and dependability of his knots. The idle hours of a long and monotonous voyage were often spent practicing what came to be known as "marlinespike seamanship"—the art of nautical knotting. Besides mastering the everyday working knots of their trade, sailors became highly skilled at tying ornamental knots for amusement and decoration. Ornamental knotting reached its peak as an art in the hands of eighteenth- and nineteenth-century seamen.

With the advent of steamships, the seaman's knotting skills were left to those who appreciated the art. Younger seamen were ignorant of all but a few basic work knots, although I managed to meet a few old salts who continued to practice this craft and were willing to pass on their knowledge—but not all of it. Each man had a few special knots, objects of great pride, that he wouldn't show anyone how to make. There was a fierce competition among knotters, and it wasn't easy to duplicate an especially intricate knot.

Demonstrated step by step on the pages that follow are a few of the knots that I have found to be the most useful, versatile, and dependable. (I have even included one that I invented—not an easy thing to do in view of the fact that man has been tying knots since before the dawn of history.) In addition, there are a number of ornamental projects that are all based on that single simple and handsome knot, the carrick bend.

Opposite: An array of knotted festoonery for indoors and out—including planter hangings, a wall hanging, and a driftwood wall decoration with a nautical theme—shows the kinds of practical and decorative uses you can find for the knotting skills described on the pages that follow.

John Hensel is an authority on nautical knotting and the author of four books on the subject, among them The Book of Ornamental Knots *and the* Encyclopedia of Knots and Fancy Rope Work *(with Raoul Graumont). He has conducted knotting workshops at the New York Botanical Gardens. An avid sailor and fisherman, he is a member of the South Fork Craftsmen's Guild near his home on eastern Long Island.*

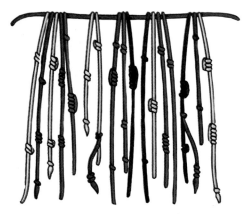

The Incas of Peru lacked a written language, but they devised this quipu (pronounced key-poo)—an ingenious arithmetical calculator based on a series of knots—to record important facts and events and enable them to keep records of commerce throughout their empire. To a main cord were attached and knotted smaller vari-colored cords, each having a special significance.

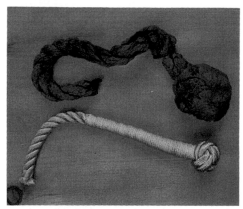

The large, partially decomposed manrope knot (top), circa 1725, was probably part of a gangway handrail. The fistlike terminal knot kept the rope from slipping through the small eyes that held it to supporting stanchions. When splicing new rigging at dockside, sailors would throw the old materials overboard, and this one—of tarred hemp—lay in the mud on New York's waterfront for 250 years, until it was found by Dr. Theodore Kazimiroff. Below it is a modern example of the same knot made from nylon rope.

According to legend, sailors of antiquity bought magic knots from sorcerers in the belief that favorable winds could be tied up in such knots and released during a calm, as depicted in this print, which accompanied a Latin text published in 1677.

Practical Knots

You don't have to be a cowboy, a sailor, or an Indian fakir to make a length of rope behave. You can easily master a few basic knots that will do dozens of everyday jobs. Any scrap of ordinary work rope will do for practicing. Or, for that matter, you can use venetian blind cord, clothesline, twine, string, or even fishing line.

When you move on to decorative projects such as those that begin on page 1788, you will need the tools and materials shown in photograph 1. I recommend that you use a synthetic-fiber rope; it is more expensive than manila or jute, but it is stronger and more weather resistant, and it follows the curves of the knot better. The diameter, color, and length of rope you use are yours to choose, but keep in mind the fact that you can enhance rope designs by combining cordages of contrasting diameters and colors.

Marine suppliers, hardware stores, and crafts supply houses stock a variety of cordage materials.

1: Ropeworking tools and materials include (clockwise from right): scissors and knife for cutting rope; hammer and small nails to fasten designs to a surface; pins for keeping the rope in place during knotting; an assortment of ropes and yarns; a tape measure; needle and thread to sew ends out of sight in a design; cellophane tape to keep rope ends from unraveling; and reference books for selecting the right knot for the job.

The Square Knot

The square knot is used for joining two pieces of rope securely. It works best when both are of the same thickness.

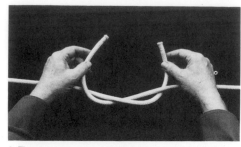

2: Entwine the ropes with both hands and point the ends away from you, left end over and right end under the ropes being joined.

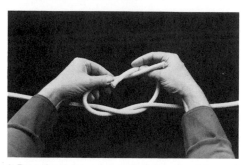

3: Pass the right end over the left end and through the resulting loop.

4: Pull both rope ends to tighten the knot.

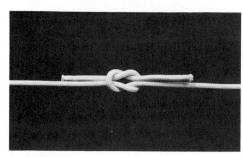

5: The finished knot consists of two opposing loops that keep each other from slipping.

The Figure-of-Eight with Half Hitches

This is a good knot combination for tying a package. A well-tied knot is easier to untie than a tangled assortment of random knots. (A heavier rope than is ordinarily used for package tying is shown here for illustration purposes, but a large ornamental knot should not be overlooked as a finishing touch for a specially wrapped present.)

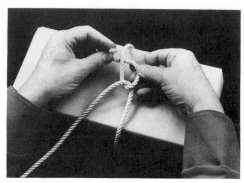

6: Entwine the width of the package with the rope, and pass the short working end under the other end and under itself.

7: Form the figure 8 by passing the working end behind and up through the loop. Pull to tighten.

8: Bring the rope lengthwise around the package, and pass the new working end under the cross rope close to the knot.

9: Make a half hitch by bringing the working end over and back under the rope beyond the knot; then pass the working end over itself.

10: Pull the rope to tighten the half hitch.

11: Make another half hitch on the opposite side of the knot by passing the working end under and back over the lengthwise rope, then under itself.

12: Pull the rope tight, cut off the excess cordage, and you have a securely tied package.

The Trucker's Hitch

Used as a load binder on open trucks, this knot increases the rope leverage by as much as 75 percent. It is a good knot to use for tying down a tent or anything else requiring a taut line that can be untied quickly.

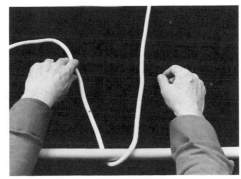

13: Pass the end of the rope over the object it is being tied to, then with your left hand, back under the object.

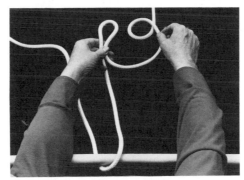

14: Double, but do not loop, the right-hand rope with your left hand, and farther to the right, make a loop with your right hand.

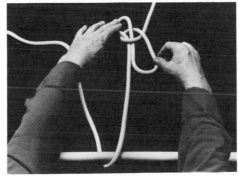

15: Insert the doubled section of rope through the loop, creating the new loop held by the right hand in the photograph.

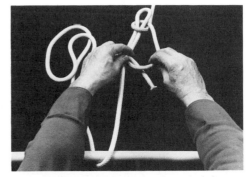

16: Turning to the free end of rope on the left, pass it through the new loop from above.

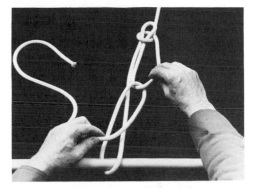

17: Pass the new working end across the stationary ropes, forming yet another loop.

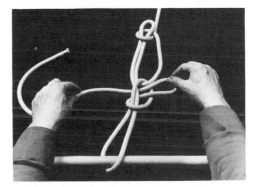

18: Thread a doubled section of the working rope back through the newest loop.

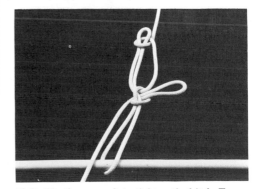

19: Pull both rope ends to tighten the hitch. To untie, simply pull the free end of the rope.

The Clove Hitch

The clove hitch is one of the most useful knots when you need to tie a rope to something. This is the knot cowboys use for tethering their horses to a hitching post.

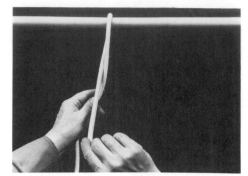

20: Pass the working end of the rope (in right hand) over the object, and pull it forward.

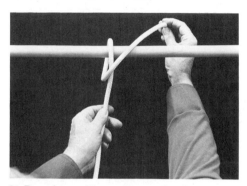

21: Pass the working end across the stationary end and back over the object.

22: Bring the working end forward, and thread it up behind itself through the V-shaped gap in front of the object and to the right of the first loop.

23: Pull both rope ends to tighten the knot around the object.

The Fast Bowline

With 3,800 known knots in existence, the odds against inventing a new one are overwhelming. But here's one I came up with myself. Because it's like the traditional bowline (pronounced bolin) knot and is very secure, I call it the fast bowline. Since it neither slips nor jams, I find it especially useful for mooring, hoisting and securing a line to the clew (lower corner) of a sail.

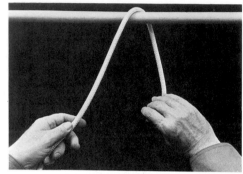

24: Pass the right-hand end of the rope over the object.

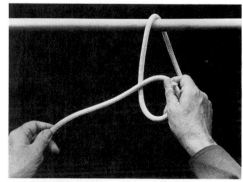

25: Form a loop in the other end of the rope near the object.

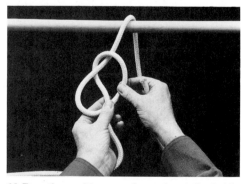

26: Pass the working rope (here, the section held in the left hand) behind, but not through, the loop. Hold the left thumb over the lower rope intersection.

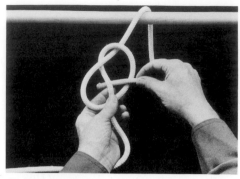

27: Now the right-hand rope becomes the working rope. Weave it across the loop, passing it first over the right side of the loop, then under the rope held beneath the loop.

28: Continue weaving the working end, passing it over the left side of the loop. Then pull the end toward you.

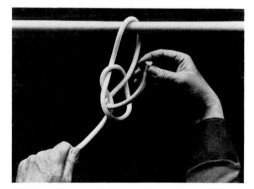

29: Snap the attached rope downward to the left and the free end of rope upward to the right.

30: The fast bowline is securely tied.

Ornamental Knots

Any of the knots already described could be used, alone or in combinations, as the basis for a decorative project. But some knots are visually more interesting than others. The projects that follow are based on the carrick bend (Figure A), an attractive and symmetrical knot of great versatility in ornamental rope work. You can begin by making a decorative accessory to wear while you master the technique of making this knot; then go on to the more complex projects that follow—a doubled carrick-bend chain mounted on a driftwood plaque, a hot-plate pad, and a hanging planter.

Preparing the Work Surface

Since the ornamental designs employ several knot combinations, pin your work to a surface so you can avoid losing the shape of the knot. A cloth-covered cork board or a square of ceiling tile will serve. Pin the rope in place as you complete each step. Besides holding the knots in place, the pins will help you keep track of loose ends. For me, T pins are easier on the fingers than regular straight pins.

A
Figure A: The carrick bend—sometimes called the sailor's breastplate knot—consists of two intertwined loops of rope. It is used to tie the air hose lines of a diving suit when they are not in use.

The Carrick Bend

This knot makes an attractive ornament either alone or in combination with other knots. With smaller cordage, it can be used as a decorative accessory for hats and clothing. The instructions that follow are for making a doubled carrick bend on a bight—that is, the knot is made with a pair of parallel ropes and is tied from both ends of a center point (the bight of a rope). You will need one piece of rope 3½ feet long and another piece 4½ feet long.

31: Pair the ropes with the longer one away from you, arranging them in an inverted V shape; then pin them down at the midpoint.

32: Form a loop with the right halves, passing the working ends over themselves. Don't let the parallel ropes cross each other.

33: Bring the left ropes under the center of the loop, and secure them with pins at both crossing points. A triple loop is thus formed.

34: Pass the left working ends over the right ends and then under the fixed ropes just to the right of the bight (the pinned midpoint).

35: Continue weaving the left working ends across the triple loop, passing them first over, then under, and finally over the next three rope intersections.

36: Pull the slack through the final loop, and remove all but the first pins.

37: Tighten and even off the ropes so the distance between the pinned bight and the center of the knot equals the larger diameter of the knot.

Carrick bend chain

Once you have learned to make the doubled carrick bend on a bight (page 1787), many decorative effects are possible. The ornamental wall plaque pictured (below right) requires more rope than the previous project but little more skill. To make it, you will need two pieces of three-strand ⅜-inch rope, each 13 feet long, and a few small nails to fasten the finished work to its backing.

38: After making a doubled carrick bend on a bight (page 1787), form a loop with the left ends, passing the ends over themselves. Make the loop about twice as far from the bight as the first knot, and pin the ropes where they cross.

39: Bring the right ends under the center of the loop, thus forming a triple loop. Pin at the intersections; then bring the right ends over the left ones.

40: Make a final pass with the working ends (these were the right ends but are now at the upper left), weaving them back across the triple loop in an under-over-under-over sequence.

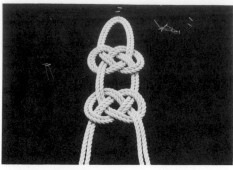

41: Pull up the slack and even off the ropes so the second knot is the same size as the first knot. Remove all the pins but the top ones.

42: Begin the third knot by again forming a loop with the left ends, but this time pass the working ends under themselves. Pin at the intersection.

43: Bring the right ends over the center of the loop to form another triple loop. Pin the intersections, and bring the right ends under the left ones.

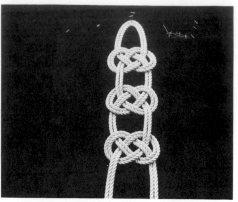

44: Again make the final pass from the upper left, but this time reverse the weave—over-under-over-under. Adjust the ropes so all three knots are evenly spaced and equally tight. Remove all pins and mount the finished work with small nails on a piece of driftwood. Trim any uneven ends.

Mounted on a piece of driftwood, a chain of knots makes an interesting wall decoration.

Weaving, Braiding, and Knotting
Hot-plate pad ¢ ⊠ 👫 🎒

Most knots when tightened take on a lumpy three-dimensional form. The usefulness of the carrick bend is increased by the fact that it can be tightened, like a woven textile, to form a reasonably flat surface. You can take advantage of this in using the knot to make place mats, doormats, belts, and other flat objects. A 9-inch hot-plate pad like the ones shown (top right) requires a 14-foot length of ½-inch rope, plus a needle and heavy thread for sewing the rope ends out of sight.

47: Pull up the slack each time the working end emerges from the knot; then continue to weave.

The eminently practical carrick-bend knot can be used to make hot-plate pads, as well as coasters, napkin rings, and place mats.

45: Make a single-strand carrick bend (see photographs 31 to 37, page 1787). Form the knot a few inches from the left end of the rope, rather than at its center, leaving the right rope end much longer.

48: The final loop is woven alongside the first strand to complete the second pass.

50: On completing the third pass, pull up the slack and even off the knot. Be sure the tripled ropes parallel each other without crossing at any point.

46: Double the knot by weaving the long end back through it. Begin from the left end and run the working rope just to the outside of the loops of the first carrick bend.

49: Weave in a third parallel pass as you did the second, following the sequence in photographs 46 to 48.

51: Turn the completed knot over and sew each rope end to the adjacent rope, thus keeping the knot tight and the ends out of sight when the hot-plate pad is in use. Cut off any excess rope.

Right: Stirrups and knotted rope are combined to support a swinglike shelf for bottles. If you scour the attic, comb the beach at ebb tide, and follow local rummage sales, you can find many interesting relics which can be incorporated into rope work.

Far right: The possibilities of ornamental knotting are limited only by the imagination. Here, 175 feet of nylon rope and five different knots, including many variations of the carrick bend, were used in tying this 5-foot-high ship's anchor. The knot in the lower right corner, called a dragonfly, is the craftsman's signature knot.

Planters and bird feeding stations, suspended with knotted ropes from an eave or bough, decorate a suburban yard (left) or beach-front patio (right). Terrariums and fish bowls can be similarly suspended.

Weaving, Braiding, and Knotting
Knotted planter hanging

¢ ⬛ 👫 🔥

For me, the most satisfying rope works are those in which the ropes and knots have a practical function, for fastening, suspending, binding, and so on. Hammocks, netting, rope handrails, swings, and planter hangings are a few of the obvious possibilities that are more than merely decorative. To make the planter hanging shown (top right), you need four pieces of ¼-inch rope, each 12 feet long, and a tape measure. Since the hanging is three-dimensional, it's a good idea to have a simple working sketch (Figure B) as a reference. If you want to make a hanging of a different design or size, modify the diagram accordingly. You can, of course, substitute any knots you like for the carrick bends indicated, assuming they will hold securely. For four other planter-hanging ideas, refer to the illustrations opposite and on page 1783. For related crafts and projects, see "Macramé" and "Hammocks and Slings."

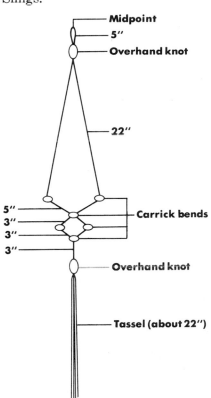

B
Figure B: The sketch for a planter hanging shows the locations of all knots and the lengths of all intervening rope spans. Instructions follow for making this one. If you make a mistake, you have wasted nothing but time; just untie the knots and start over.

Labels in Figure B: Midpoint, 5", Overhand knot, 22", 5", 3", 3", 3", Carrick bends, Overhand knot, Tassel (about 22")

52: With a piece of cord, tie all four ropes together at their midpoint.

53: Holding the midpoint in one hand and the eight strands (of the four doubled ropes) in the other, tie an overhand knot just below the midpoint.

C
Figure C: The overhand knot is the most basic and familiar knot of all (though not everyone knows its name). To make it, loop the rope over itself; then thread the end through the loop from behind.

You can make a plant hanging with a series of carrick bends, tied off with an overhand knot.

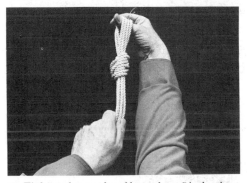

54: Tighten the overhand knot about 5 inches below the tied midpoint of the ropes.

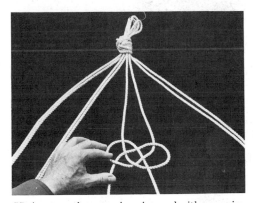

55: Arrange the ropes in pairs, and with one pair, tie a carrick bend (photographs 31 to 37, page 1787) 22 inches below the overhand knot.

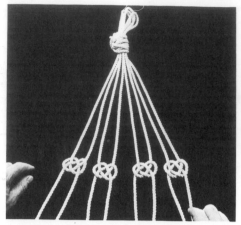

56: Tighten the first knot; then tie and tighten carrick bends with each of the three remaining rope pairs. Locate all four knots the same distance below the overhand knot.

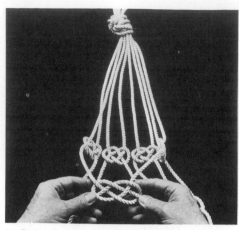

59: Bring the two remaining ropes, one at each side, forward. Tie them together to complete the second series of carrick bends. The hanger now begins to take on a three-dimensional aspect.

62: Collect all the rope ends and tie them together with an overhand knot 3 inches below the last series of carrick bends.

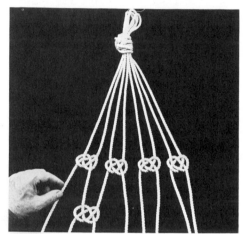

57: Holding the left rope aside, tie another carrick bend 5 inches below the first series, this time using the second and third ropes from the left.

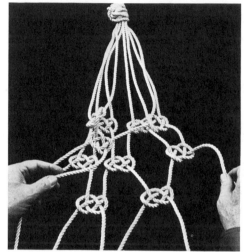

60: Make a third series of carrick bends 3 inches below the second series. Again alternate the pairing of the ropes so the staggered pattern continues.

63: Unravel the strands below the overhand knot to create a tassel effect. Cut off any rope ends that protrude below the tassel effect. Cut off any rope ends that protrude below the tassel. Suspend the hanger and put a decorative plant holder in the rope basket you have made.

58: Pair the fourth rope with the fifth, and the sixth with the seventh, in tying additional carrick bends, also located 5 inches below the first series.

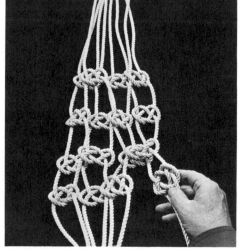

61: Continuing to alternate the pairing of the ropes, make the fourth and final row of knots 3 inches below the third series.